DOG THAT SAVED ME

By
CAPTAIN TOM TOLER

Printed in the United States of America

ISBN: 9781688221864

First Trade paperback edition in 2019.

Author Consultant and Editing: Company 614 Enterprises, LLC
Cover Artwork and Design: Tawni Franzen at ayaristudio.com
Text Design and Composition: Rick Soldin

All photos from the Tom Toler Family Collection used with permission. Jimmy Stewart photo with permission of Harry Benson.

Paperback Printed by Amazon – Kindle Direct Publishing
eBook distributed by Amazon – Kindle Direct Publishing

Jimmy Stewart™ used with permission from The Stewart Family, LLC.

This is a true story. The names of some characters, locations, and situations have been changed.

"…and done a hundred things you have never dreamed of," in the Introduction is from the poem "High Flight" by John Gillespie Magee, Jr.

To Big T, my larger-than-life father. You
  gave me the opportunity to achieve,
  which is way more than most young boys
  get. I hope you were proud of me.

To my former wife, Donna. You gave me the
  love I craved, but I disappointed you way
  too often. I hope you can forgive me.

To my bestest buddy, Duke. You brought
  me back from the dead, giving me a
  reason to live. And live we did!

Contents

Introduction

Over a decade ago, a young vet named Tracy Sackman suggested I write a book about my dog Duke. She thought the story should be told as if Duke was telling his experience of suffering, hunger, abuse, and rescue—a tale of what it's like to pass through the doors of hell—only to find redemption, security, safety, and love. I thought she had a pretty good idea.

When I first saw my little boy, he was hiding in a corner, shaking and panting. I found a chair and sat down where I could get a good look at him. After studying him for a few minutes, I patted my knees and said, "It's okay, boy, I've gotcha." He blinked a few times, looked me over, then bolted over, trying hard to jump up in my lap. But he needed help. I firmly picked him up, held his scrawny body for a few moments, and stared into his hazel-brown eyes. "I'll be back for you," I said with conviction. "Don't worry, I've gotcha."

For most of my life I was goal oriented, determined to achieve everything possible in business and commercial aviation at the earliest age allowable. My first solo flight on my sixteenth birthday was at night—a first according to Cessna research. Since then, I've flown for the rich and famous, captained White House charters, survived a 9/11 scare, and served twenty-eight years with American Airlines before obtaining my USCG Master Captain sea license. I can say truthfully that over my life, I've lived hard "...and done a hundred things you have never dreamed of."* So why write a book about a dog named Duke?

---

*From the poem "High Flight" by John Gillespie Magee, Jr.

I had never claimed to be a dog lover, even though my family always had dogs. My wife, Donna, and I had three Welsh Corgis at one point. But they were never my dogs. When I met Duke, he was *my* dog, *my* buddy. Together, we survived near-death experiences, each of us given a ten percent chance to live. We were both given up on, yet together we beat the odds.

Duke was a handsome Australian Blue Heeler mix. His piercing eyes complemented the white accents of his thick navy-blue coat. I could look in his eyes and see both the pain of having to dodge so many of life's curve balls and the joy of finally landing in Shangri-la. His courage was contagious, and it taught me to appreciate the one simple and important fact of life: it's not all about me.

I loved Duke with all my heart and soul. So this has been a painful and emotional book to write. But it makes me smile knowing we gave each other a better life. There will never be another Duke, but God willing, he will remain in the memories of so many that he touched.

Captain Tom

Chapter One

January 2015

I had been flying since I was twelve—for more than fifty years. And in all that time and all those flights, only once had I faced the possibility of crashing and dying. A single-engine Comanche 250 was involved. So was a cute blonde copilot who would eventually have a hit play on Broadway. I was twenty-two and quickly put it behind me. Now, at sixty-two, I was having my second introduction to death. Only this time, I wasn't in the air.

We had set out from Panama City in the *Prima D*—a forty-three-foot Hatteras motor yacht. She was my boat and I was her captain.

Before we left, I'd checked the weather report. It looked good enough to cut the corner on the upper west coast of Florida. From the horn of Saint Joseph Bay across the Gulf to Clearwater, I would save a lot of time.

Based on my nautical maps and experience of other boaters, the trip would take no more than twelve hours. Really, it was going to be easy, especially for a Coast Guard Certified Master like me. Yet as we rounded the horn and headed out to open sea, I noticed the burgee shift. Instead of having the wind (and the waves) at my back, the blue and white pennant shifted about an hour into the trip. Now the wind came from the northeast, pushing my port (left) side over and submerging the starboard (right) gunnels in the frothy sea. Each time the *Prima D* rolled over, it rocked back into place. And each time, I swallowed hard.

Where is this coming from? I thought.

The pressure was dropping, telling me that a storm was coming. That was easy to see as the sun dipped over the western horizon, lighting up the approaching clouds. Whatever it was, I didn't want to be in it.

I rubbed my jaw and considered the options. We were no more than two hours from Apalachicola. To head back, I'd have to turn south and ease my way to the west before I could dare turn north. That would probably be the best option.

A wave crashed into the flybridge above me, sending a thin spray through the windscreen. It stung my face. I blinked a few times and considered the implications.

The flybridge deck is eighteen feet above the ocean. How the hell did that just happen?

Studying the muddy Gulf, I estimated I had five-to-seven-foot seas. When the outlying nine-foot waves joined forces, it produced an occasional eighteen-foot wave. That was supposed to be rare—like once an hour. Yet I could see more eighteen-footers were on the way. Turning back into these monsters would not only be hard, but dumb.

I had to consider the other option: continue heading toward Clearwater—maybe edge north of that—and hope I could outrun the storm. I had plenty of fuel, and Randy Cotter could switch fuel tanks. Right now, Randy was below deck sleeping soundly. He was a kid who managed marinas and picked up work like this. Unfortunately, his wife had recently given birth to twins. He'd been up all night taking care of them. When he arrived late at the marina, we didn't clear Panama City until five p.m. This put us behind by nine hours—time that might be the difference between life and death.

I stood on the wheelhouse deck, looking at my GPS navigator and course plotter. For some reason, it wasn't working. My backup navigation system—the gyrocompass—was spinning like a top. Whenever the spinning slowed, it tilted side to side, making it impossible to get a true reading. If we continued to Clearwater, it would take an experienced captain at the helm the entire way. I fit that bill, but there was no way I could stand for ten more hours, much less stay awake.

Then there was Randy. He had jerked the ropes from the dock in Panama City, coiled them up nicely, and crawled onto the couch in the cabin below, falling asleep and hardly moving. If the trip stayed this rough and I needed a few hours of rest, there was no way he could do it. Not in this mess. He could barely steer the *Prima D* in the perfectly calm water of the Intracoastal. Holding the rudder in five-to-seven-foot seas with waves smashing into the flybridge was beyond his abilities. Plus, this boat had a lot of bells and whistles. One wrong lever pulled and we could find ourselves in Davy Jones's locker at the bottom of the Gulf of Mexico.

A scene from a future TV show flashed through my mind. An underwater drone searched the ocean floor, finding all sorts of doomed boats and crashed planes. I could hear the narrator:

> "Here is the final resting place for the *Prima D*. It vanished without a trace in 2015, taking with it Captain Tom Toler and Randy Cotter. Also lost was Mr. Toler's dog, Duke, a Blue Heeler he'd rescued as a puppy. The Coast Guard searched for three days before finally giving up. It was just another vessel that slipped beneath the waves, forever gone. And now, we have learned her fate."

That's it! I'm turning around.

Just as I was about to spin the wheel to starboard and relieve some pressure from the rudder, I felt a bump and a lurch. I glanced at the dials and saw nothing wrong. This was distressing.

If we'd been in the Intracoastal, I would have figured we hit some debris like a log or sunken craft. But I had at least forty feet below me to the bottom. No way I could hit anything other than a whale or, God forbid, a great white shark. And no sense letting my mind wander to that. I didn't need to be thinking about Jaws climbing into the tiny dinghy with Duke and Randy. We'd be sitting there, waiting for another twenty-foot wave to topple us over. Then we'd float in our life vests until something removed our feet and legs one at a time.

The boat started pulling to starboard and the speed seemed to slow. I glanced at the controls. Nothing indicated a problem. To compensate for the obvious pull, I turned the wheel to port, feeling resistance from the increased pressure on the rudder. If I wasn't careful, I could snap the rudder off, leaving the *Prima D* to founder on the waves. In no time, the boat would capsize, and we'd be in the dinghy until *it* capsized. Then the leg and feet nightmare would become a reality.

I ran my hands over my face and reevaluated the options. With the wind and waves insisting I head south toward Cuba or Cancun, I'd run out of fuel long before I saw land down there. Running out of fuel on the seas meant only one thing: waiting for a wave to capsize you. That replayed the dinghy and *Jaws* movie in my head. In fact, I couldn't get it to stop. I was in a terrible jam.

I ran through the options again before making fuel capacity the deciding factor. I had to hit land before I ran out of fuel. Plain and simple. I'd have to aim for the west coast of Florida and pray I could make it.

I fired up the GPS chart plotter and discovered it still didn't work. Turning on the light behind me, I saw the fishtailed wake of the *Prima D*. I was all over the place. No wonder the GPS navigation system didn't work. Even the gyrocompass whirled around like I was in the Bermuda Triangle. As my mind combed through these problems for answers, I felt a nip at my left heel. Looking down, I saw Duke.

"What is it, boy?" I asked.

When he nipped me again, I felt adrenaline shoot through my veins. I'd been up early getting the boat ready, shorting myself of much-needed sleep. With the late start, I faced an all-nighter to reach Clearwater. If I was going to make it, I'd need help staying awake.

Is that what you're doing? You're going to keep me awake?

Duke seemed to nod. Of course, it could have been the rocking of the boat. It was hard to tell.

A massive wave crashed over the flybridge, stunning me again. The nightmare was here.

My mind spun in five directions. Then I spotted the red emergency button above me.

"That's it!" I yelled. "It's time to call for help."

I had forgotten all about the red button. The *Prima D*'s wheelhouse was loaded with lots of goodies. This button was one of them. Simply push it and a mayday beamed out on all frequencies along with the GPS coordinates. Thank God for technology.

"Help's on the way," I told Duke as I flipped back the plastic protector.

Scanning the gauges one last time, I wanted to be sure. Every Coast Guard rescue could lead to an inquiry. That meant sworn testimony. I didn't need to be caught in some inconsistency. After confirming this was my only option, I pressed the button.

The Coast Guard training had taught me that right now, nearby vessels were receiving my distress call. Some captain somewhere was reviewing this information and determining how far he was from my boat. Any second now, he would pick up the radio and call me. All I had to do was keep the boat afloat until he arrived.

I stood there watching the waves roll over my port side, splashing water all over the deck. Every few seconds, I glanced at the radio to make sure it was working. It was.

After fifteen minutes of nothing, I pressed the red button again. Time crawled by. Surely, a Coast Guard station in proximity would call. Yet after thirty full minutes, I hadn't received a call from anyone.

How can this be?

I thought for a moment. In taking this boat from Texas to Clearwater, Florida, I had put in at Mobile, Alabama, for repairs. The marina there had screwed up so bad I had to get a lawyer involved.

Eventually, I received $20,000 back on my credit card along with their guarantee that they would fix everything, including the GPS navigation system. However, they weren't supposed to touch the emergency button.

I recalled how I had hammered the owner with legal threats and appeals on my American Express. Everyone had sided with me, costing him a lot of money and a good chunk of his reputation. The owner had been pissed, but finally agreed to the settlement—part of which was to deliver the boat to Panama City. I figured if the repairs weren't done right, the boat would break down on the way. It was a good plan, but not a great one. I stood in the wheelhouse considering its flaws.

The owner could have run the *Prima D* in the Intracoastal on idle speed. This would have avoided testing the engines and propeller shafts. And they wouldn't have needed the navigation system since they made the trip in one day with clear weather. Reading maps and seeing buoys would have been a cinch.

I lowered my head at the next thought. They could have been so pissed that they pulled a wire on the emergency mayday system. In fact, my "good" plan was an invitation to screw me. And how could I sue them when I was at the bottom of the Gulf of Mexico?

No, they had a great plan—it was called *payback*. The more I turned it over, the more I was sure they had screwed me. I could only pray to God that the damage was limited to my starboard engine, GPS navigation system, and emergency red button. If I could keep the other engine going, I still had a chance to make it to dry land. But that was a big if.

Duke nipped at me again.

"Okay, I get it," I said. "You're going to do your part and keep me alert and awake."

I looked at my watch. 8:30 p.m. The sky was covered with clouds. If it stayed like this, I wouldn't have the stars to steer by. With no functioning navigational system, the stars were my only hope.

"All right, Duke, you stay vigilant and keep me awake. I swear to you, I'll do my best to get us to land."

Duke stared up at me.

I took a sip from my water bottle and sighed. "How about I tell you some stories? That way, you won't have to keep nipping at my heel."

Hearing this, Duke sat, his tongue contentedly hanging out.

"Okay. Let's start with my dad. Did you know he was in the Grand Prairie Mafia? No? Let me tell you all about it. I think we have plenty of time."

Chapter Two

Sure, my dad was in the mafia. It wasn't like the normal mob you see in movies, but it was close. I guess it's no surprise that I tried to follow in his footsteps.

My criminal career kicked off with a bang when I worked my way up to an inside position of trust. I used it to pull off a heist that would later be known as the A-Bomb Caper. They still talk about it today—at least, the ones still alive.

The heist took place at Glenview Elementary in Richland Hills, a suburb of Fort Worth. I was a decent student in the fourth grade, always well-dressed and polite. I leveraged this façade to be selected as a patrol boy. This was an important position in the life of an elementary student. I was responsible for getting the other children across the street safely. The job involved raising bright orange flags that hung from bamboo poles to stop traffic.

This honor also came with a bright orange sash and large badge to display my authority. As I slipped it over my thin frame for the first time, the experience took my breath away. I was somebody to be reckoned with. I had power, and I intended to use it.

Besides the badge and sash, the position came with a key benefit: early morning access to the school. This was the true prize.

For the first week, I let things sort out, getting the lay of the land. I committed the exterior security guards' schedule to memory. Once I felt comfortable, it was time to explore. First up was my grammar class.

Each Friday, we had a grammar test from the *Weekly Reader*. I had been making As and Bs, but was never able to reach a perfect score. During my second week as patrol boy, I hit the mother lode. Right there on the teacher's desk were the test questions and answers just begging to be copied down. I could almost hear them saying, "Come on, Tom, take us with you." So I did.

The first week, I hit a perfect score. I discovered that taking tests was easy when you had the answers. From then on, I arrived at school early each Friday. I went to my locker and put on my sash and badge. Then I snuck into my grammar class to steal the answers.

One day, two patrol buddies in my class wondered what I was doing. I let them in on my find.

Why not?

Give everyone a chance to wet their beak.

I knew that with my previous record of an occasional A, my perfect score wouldn't set off any alarms. So I made a perfect score each week. It was a flawless caper.

Well, almost.

You see, every crime is only as strong as its weakest member. One man cracks, one man slips up, and they can roll on the others. That's what went through my mind one morning as my two patrol boy buddies and I huddled over the teacher's desk, copying the answers like a pack of jackals feeding on a downed zebra. Suddenly, the classroom door behind us slammed shut. As I slowly turned around, I spotted the teacher glaring at me. The principal stood next to her, angrily tapping a long paddle against his right thigh. Oh man, I was so busted.

As I grabbed my ankles, absorbing the repeated impact of a quarter-inch-thick plank of wood, I learned that one of my buddies usually bombed the weekly test. When he'd suddenly pulled off a perfect score, the teacher knew something was up. She'd expected to catch one rat. She was overjoyed to find three.

With my patrol boy status unceremoniously stripped from my young chest, I rode home on my bike with a note for Dad to sign. I had to lean on my arms and stand on the pedals to keep my aching butt off the seat. It felt like a death ride.

Each evening, Dad trudged in from a long day of running his crew. He was exhausted. The last thing he needed was more problems. That's why he relaxed, undid his belt, and used it to whip the criminality out of me. The rest is pretty hazy. For sure there was some crying and enough injuries to convict a parent for child abuse in today's world.

After that experience, I decided a life of crime was not the way to go. Maybe if I could've started at the top like Dad, I might have stayed. Instead, I kept my nose clean and never looked back.

Before I was born, there were some important people in my soon-to-be life. Robbie Helen King was one of them. Helen had done some modeling in her early days. She was a looker. Helen met Dad in high school. After graduation they married on the Bride and Groom Radio Program—something everyone listened to. Not surprisingly, the program featured great-looking people. This was important because the producers followed each show up with newspaper articles and photos, hoping to sell wedding services.

Mom was a gracious lady, always dolled up like June Cleaver—a smart dress, pearls, and classy shoes. She awoke early each morning to properly apply her makeup and fix her hair, remaining in perfect condition until it was time for bed. I never saw her looking casual or without makeup.

Dad's story was a bit different. After high school and marriage, he joined the Navy. Somehow, he became an officer, learning to fly planes. He also dove into the mechanics of how planes operated. When he came home, he attended SMU and earned an electrical engineering degree. Afterward, he was a top engineer for Convair on the B36 bombardier doors. He was fairly smart.

Grimes Manufacturing Company, in Urbana, Ohio, plucked him out and set him on his way to fame and fortune. Grimes made lights that were well-known in the aircraft industry. Before Grimes, pilots used flashlights to see instruments and read charts. When Warren Grimes invented the red and green navigation lights for wingtips on aircraft, he expanded to the cockpit, creating tiny lights that shone over each instrument. The Grimes light became standard in every plane until much later, when integrated lighted instruments came along. But during the Grimes heyday, it was a great place to be.

Dad was a Grimes manufacturer's rep, responsible for the West Coast and Southwest territory. On straight commission, he was essentially self-employed.

Dad traveled all the time, selling Grimes lighting systems to aircraft manufacturers and anyone else who wanted them. This included companies that made boats, trains, and cars. But because Dad had grown up poor, he wanted something else. What he wanted was *more*. More money. More stuff. More life.

He set up his operation, Control Engineering, in Richland Hills, Texas. This was a few miles from a place called Grand Prairie. When you first hear the name, it sounds like a Kansas wheat field. Incredibly, it was a strategic spot in the middle of the country where many of World War II's aircraft were manufactured. Companies like North American Aviation, Chance Vought Aviation, Temco, James Ling Electronics, and the merged conglomerate of Ling-Temco-Vought— LTV—cranked out aircraft and aircraft parts. Tens of thousands of factory workers punched in each day somewhere in Grand Prairie. That was a lot of potential for a man who could see it. And Thomas Willard Toler could see it.

Big T, a nickname he soon earned, had a large personality to match. Men respected him because he knew when and how to use his power. Big T found a way to wiggle his finger into every pie. One revenue stream involved certified aircraft parts. Each one has a Technical Standard Order (TSO) number. TSO numbers drive up the price of aircraft parts, making them expensive. That's why Big T had two friends selling non-TSO parts in hydraulics and electronics. It was very profitable. For example, if a new TSO hydraulic strut sold for $5,000, a non-TSO part might sell for $2,500. If a seller's cost was $1,000, he could turn a nice profit.

Using Big T's connections at the factories, these "friends" did well. When Big T's friends did well, so did Big T.

With his legitimate Grimes lighting business and his under-the-table income, Dad did well. So well that he needed a secretary. Marilyn Crenshaw appeared out of nowhere and began running Dad's professional life. As his business expanded, Dad bought fourplexes, moving his office into one of them. Eventually, Marilyn became more than a secretary.

Now back to me—Big T's son, Tom Earl Toler. I was always dressed in a coat and tie. "Looking good!" I said each morning as I stared into the mirror. I rarely wore jeans, instead maintaining the image of a clean-cut fraternity boy who would probably run for office.

When my younger brother, Gary, and I were growing up, Mom mostly raised us. With Dad always gone, this felt normal to her. She wasn't used to having men around. Her father had died before Mom was born, having left his wife and Mom to fend for themselves. Apparently, he was some Hollywood scoundrel who worked angles; a grifter in the movie industry. I'm sure that affected her understanding of men.

For some reason, Mom never made breakfast. But at least she always looked good not making it.

Dad got up early and had breakfast at a diner. Since he came home late, he missed out on our baseball games and other events. He made up for it by paying for things. So both of my parents had good and bad traits that Gary and I adjusted to.

As for me, I discovered an early eye for the ladies. We were living in New Jersey for a brief time. I was in kindergarten. It was the first day of school and I found myself in line for some construction paper. I was standing there, checking out my new classmates, when I noticed the girl in front of me. She was easily the prettiest girl I'd ever seen in my six years on this planet. Filled with jubilation and excitement, I leaned over and kissed her on the cheek. Then I twirled my body in a full circle. Really, I flipped over this girl.

Sadly, she had standards to maintain. From that day forward, she kept an eye on me, not allowing me to kiss her again.

Even though I had that brief taste of love, it was four years later when I really fell in love. The location was a Braniff Lockheed Electra. Dad had taken me on a business trip and asked the captain if his son could come up and look in the cockpit. "Send him right on up," the captain replied.

I sprinted through the aisle, into the cockpit, where he fastened me to the jump seat. The captain spent a lot of time explaining the instruments and letting me watch everything. After what seemed like a long time, I noticed we were close to Boston. "Well, I guess I need to go on back," I said.

"No," the captain replied. "You can sit here for the landing." I rubbed my hands together as he continued. "Now, when we get there, you'll notice that there's a hump in the runway. My challenge is to land this plane right on top of the hump. That way, it'll be a real smooth landing."

As we neared the landing strip, he glanced over at me. "Okay, now, can you see that hump?"

"Oh, yeah, yeah," I replied. There wasn't any hump, but I wasn't about to blow his story. I was having too much fun.

As he touched down, he said, "That was the hump! That was the hump!" I didn't care about a hump. I thought it was the greatest thing I'd ever seen in my life. I was hooked.

From that day forward, I spent all my spare time at the airport where Dad kept his single-engine Cessna 172. When I turned twelve, he let me start flying. I did anything for money to pay for the gas to fly. Dad, ever the sharp operator, saw that I was addicted to something and used that to his advantage.

Before I could see his "inside operation," he arranged traditional work for me like mowing the grass, cleaning the toilets, and other chores at his main office. Some of the companies that were part of his "consortium" needed help. One of them stored aircraft parts. I worked there sorting out parts, storing them, and occasionally conducting an inventory. He always had something for me to do.

When it was time to get paid, he handed me the cash and said, "Take this and use it to fill up the airplane." That was fine with me.

One of the chores I loved was maintaining the airplane. I washed and cleaned it, even putting carpet in one of his later models. Between me and Marilyn Crenshaw, we kept Big T's world running. And let's face it—he was a walking ATM machine. He always had cash. At the time, I wasn't sure where it came from, but cash was king in Big T's world.

At fourteen, I earned my driver's license and was rewarded with a red 1959 Ford Sunliner convertible. I was the first person in junior high school to have an automobile and access to an airplane. Needless to say, I was very popular.

Even though I wanted to fly all the time, I did have two diversions. One was a band with my best friend, Conrad Rogers. Conrad— Shorty to me—played the guitar. I played the drums. Mike Layfield was on the bass and keyboard, and Doug Plume hit the rhythm guitar. We played a lot of local gigs to make some extra spending money. Really, Shorty and I were joined at the hip through high school.

My other diversion was football. I played left tackle on both offense and defense. I was an average player, like the rest of the players on our team. Coach Wilkerson had a unique coaching style. He'd make all the players run a mile. The player who came in last was paddled. It was usually me. But Coach Wilkerson had a soft spot. He'd let me catch my breath first before ordering me to drop my drawers. Then he reared back like a Tiger Woods drive and sent the paddle of justice down on my snow-white butt cheeks. He paddled me until they turned red.

After a game, if I'd missed a block or tackle, or jumped offsides, or got flagged for holding, or didn't give enough effort, I got paddled. One day, a buddy whispered to me that some guy who looked exactly like me had run off with the coach's wife. I don't know if that was true, but Coach sure loved whipping my butt. In today's world, he'd just be getting out of prison.

At night, when I wasn't playing in the band, I'd sneak out and drive to Mangham Field to watch the planes land. They had to dodge high electrical lines, which made it exciting. To me, watching the flashing lights of the airport was fascinating.

After plane watching, my buddies and I went to the nearby Jack in the Box and hung out. One night, I was detained by the police. Fortunately, I had connections. They called Dad up, and at first, he didn't want to take me back. The cops let him blow off some steam before he opened the door and let me back into his life. Still, he kept a strong eye on me for a long time.

Despite my arrest, I was finally able to start logging my flight time at fifteen. I had plenty of hours by the time I turned sixteen, the youngest age a pilot can fly solo. Cessna sent a representative to the Great Southwest Airport to watch my first supervised solo, which I made at night with no one else in the cockpit. They were stunned at my experience level.

When I turned seventeen, I wanted my private pilot's license. I had to demonstrate at least two cross-country flights of twenty-five miles or more, plus a certain number of nighttime hours. I had done all that, so I received my private license immediately.

Although my youth may have seemed idyllic, there were a few road bumps. One of which was a ski boat that appeared at our house one day. I asked Dad what kind it was and he said, "It's a Slickcraft." I knew that Slickcraft were built in Oklahoma. I also knew his secretary, Marilyn Crenshaw, was from Ardmore—right near where they built those boats. I figured he knew someone at that factory and had scored a good deal.

Later that summer, my brother, Gary, and I were running the boat on a nearby lake, skiing and having fun. Then the engine quit. I pulled off the hatch and got down there, looking around the engine with a flashlight. After a few minutes of poking around, I discovered it was not a Slickcraft but a Sea Ray. And Sea Rays were not made in Oklahoma. I knew my father was very intelligent and knew his equipment. That's why my suspicions were raised.

I started paying attention to where the boat was stored. At first, Dad kept it covered up and in a shed hidden behind his office complex. When one of his partners had a warehouse in Grand Prairie, the boat was taken there, away from prying eyes.

That hot boat was followed by a beautiful, full-length mink coat. One afternoon, Dad came home and handed it to Mom. She was thrilled. I got to looking at it and noticed its name tag had been cut out. I guess you could say Mom had a stolen stole.

But then, my attention shifted to Marilyn Crenshaw. It dawned on me that Dad was closer to her than he should be. In fact, I realized he was having an affair with her. That's when I went berserk, throwing a brick through Dad's windshield. When he confronted me, I told him my suspicions. His answer is ingrained in my mind. "Son, you don't know what you're talking about. Maybe someday you'll understand."

That someday never came.

Chapter Three

Somewhat exhausted, I struggled to remain standing at the wheel. My eyes strained against the darkness, trying to see ahead as the endless procession of white-tipped waves crashed against the *Prima D*. If a wave lifted the boat, I had to make sure we landed on the backside safely. This required expert steering and small rudder adjustments to shift the bow to port or starboard to avoid a broadside. If I spotted the wave far enough in advance, I could point the bow to slice perpendicularly through the wave. This not only minimized the lift but kept the spray off the wheelhouse screens and windshields.

Maybe the worst of the storm is over, I thought as the waves settled for a moment. But I knew all too well that the ocean was reloading, saving up energy to send me an occasional eighteen-foot rogue wave.

How many more hours do I have until we reach the west coast of Florida? Twelve? Fifteen? Eighteen?

It was impossible to guess because I had no way of knowing our exact location. The boat's erratic movement made the GPS navigator worthless.

I leaned to my right and looked up. The sky was dark. "I guess I'll have to use the stars to navigate," I said to Duke. "If they'll appear, that is."

Fat chance, Duke's eyes seemed to say. Neither the ocean nor the sky appeared generous tonight.

I ran my hands across my face. I was sixty-two years old but I felt like eighty. I was still weak from being sick for the last two years. I didn't see how I could make it.

Then there was Randy, asleep below. Each time I thought about him relieving me, I remembered the issues he had in the Intracoastal. This boat was simply too big for him. Failure to see one large broadside and we'd roll over. At ten feet under water, forget about deploying the life raft—much less jumping off. We'd be upside down, sinking with a waterlogged *Prima D.*

I felt the remaining port engine surge and closed my eyes for a second. If that quit, we were done. Another wave crashed the flybridge, sending water below it, soaking me and Duke. He didn't seem bothered. He remained dedicated, guarding my left leg. The tiny bite mark in my brown Croc was evidence he was on duty.

"I don't know where we are," I told him, "but if I don't get some stars to navigate by, we're going to be in more trouble." I pressed the red button again. "This thing doesn't work. We'd have heard from someone by now, especially those shrimpers just off the horizon."

I thought about my life so far. It wasn't lacking for adventure. I had crossed off a lot of exciting must-dos. If this was it, I had lived a full life—although not always a happy one. The worst part was knowing Duke would die with me. I guess I should have been sad about Randy too. After all, he was a father and a husband. But I didn't know him. I knew Duke. We had been through so much. Through all my failed relationships, he was the one enduring creature who had stuck by me. It hurt me to think of failing him. Because right now, he wasn't failing me.

I stared down at his trusting, obedient face. "Do you like my stories, boy? Do you?"

He licked my leg.

"Okay. You keep me awake and I'll keep going. Where did I leave off? Oh yes, Marilyn Crenshaw."

My rage-filled attack against Dad's car felt good at the time. Perhaps I thought it might actually change things. Then I remembered the fact that I was driving Marilyn Crenshaw's old car. She was woven into our lives like a neighbor's stray poison ivy plant. The vine twisted here and there, touching parts of us that it shouldn't. My anger simply acknowledged that I couldn't do anything about it. No matter how mad I got, Dad wasn't turning Marilyn loose.

For her part, Mom never allowed the name Marilyn Crenshaw to cross her lips. Later, I learned that Mom had been involved in a fling before I was born. I heard that Dad had too. I never knew if it was two newlyweds having problems, or if they had separated and felt okay about seeing other people. Or maybe they weren't enough for each other. Whatever it was, it wasn't normal. Not back in the fifties.

While I blamed Dad, I was also reminded of a friend, Denny Stalcup. He lived down the street. Denny's father sold women's clothing and had asked my mother to model it for him. I didn't think there was anything going on, but after all I'd learned, who knew?

For any kid, thinking one of your parents is cheating on the other is disturbing. It tears at the fabric of trust and family, of safety and togetherness. It affects your own relationships down the road. After all, how can you trust anyone?

Still, through all this, Mom and Dad gave the appearance of a good marriage. They got out. They went dancing at the Caribe Club. There, the well-dressed, good-looking Tolers cleared the dance floor, putting on a performance. The two moved with ease. Dad was a smooth dancer and Mom followed his every step. People loved to come and watch them dance.

When they weren't dancing, they mingled with guests and onlookers. Dad was Big T, conducting business and holding court. Mom was fun-loving and laughed a lot. But she fully understood that Big T was the center of attention. He was *the man.*

Even though I was just a teenager, I knew the Caribe Club well. Located inside the Western Hills Inn, it was a place I often worked.

The Western Hills Inn was quite unique. Try picturing this: You're leaving California, driving to the East Coast, when you come upon this glittering city in the desert called Las Vegas. There appears to be no reason it's there. But because it is, people come.

Now travel to the Dallas–Fort Worth area. In the sixties, fifty miles separated the two cities. There was nothing of consequence between them, certainly nothing fun. But driving on Highway 183 from Dallas to Fort Worth, a tall Vegas-like sign that read "Western Hills Inn" appeared out of nowhere. It had something thirsty patrons couldn't get anywhere else: alcohol. That was, so long as you were a member of the club.

Western Hills had other first-class features. A barber shop for men was an informal boardroom for the rich and famous. Many oil and gas investments came from information exchanged there. A separate beauty shop kept the women occupied and looking good. If you needed a ride to the Greater Southwest International Airport, limousines sat waiting for passengers. Then there were the rooms—140 of them. They were plush, with a sixties-style divider separating the end of the bed and a desk/sitting area. With a few retail shops off the lobby, it had everything. And it was the center of Big T's operation.

I worked at Western Hills doing various jobs. Sheila and Chester Smith owned the catering and management concession at the Caribe Club, so Dad hit them up for a favor. They put me to work bussing tables in the club and restaurant. When the restaurant closed for the day, the kitchen stayed open late. Once the room service guys went home, I was drafted to wheel the cart up and down the halls of the B-Wing, delivering sandwiches. That's when I discovered the gambling operations.

There were high stakes poker games in one room and gin rummy in another. Big stacks of cash sat on tables filled with chips, drinks, and sandwiches. Men hunched over the green felt, intently studying their cards. A lot of money changed hands. And with each pot, Big T took his rake.

I delivered a lot of food to poker players. And airline crews too. Western Hills was home to American Airline pilots and stewardesses in training. After they attended classes during the day, they ordered room service—a lot of it. I was able to see and talk to the new pilots, learn what they were doing. They got me excited about flying.

Poker and airline training weren't the only reasons people came to Western Hills. Many patrons just came for the alcohol. The Caribe Club served drinks late. Guests loved sipping on mojitos in a tropical jungle setting. The brightly colored barstools and exotic vegetation made it seem like Cuba or Panama. The cozy candlelit tables allowed for private conversations. When a few tables were pushed together, larger get-togethers happened. For the businessmen, the Caribe Club was perfect. And if a rich family or company needed more space, just across from the lobby was a massive thousand-person-capacity ballroom. It was perfect for grand weddings or well-just-came-in parties.

Western Hills was *the* place for Mom and Dad. Marilyn Crenshaw was never there with my father. But Keller Colton was. He was a hairdresser in the beauty shop. He was also a former FBI agent and police officer. And he was Big T's enforcer. If problems rose, Keller erased them. When guys didn't pay, they saw Keller. If a lady needed her hair done, Keller was her man.

I saw Keller there but didn't spend a lot of time with him. I did know his daughter. She was ten years younger than me and I taught her how to swim during my day job as lifeguard at the pool. So I was smart enough to stay on his good side.

I'd been working at the hotel for a few months when I found myself in the B-Wing with the gamblers. To get to the B-Wing, you left the hotel and walked under a metal breezeway. It was totally separate, a place where the rules of society changed. There were women available, maybe other services too. It was also where Big T met with his crew and conducted the business of the Grand Prairie Mafia—a term I first heard there.

Each night, when I took over for the room service guys, I saw all sorts of wild things. Well-known rich men counting their cash.

Women lingering around for potential customers. I watched everything with keen interest as I delivered trays of steak sandwiches and other food orders.

Dad tried to keep me away from all this stuff, yet he needed things done. I was too young to be around the gambling even if it had been legal. And I was definitely too young to set foot in the Caribe Club—you had to be twenty-one back then. But I needed a job. Because Big T wasn't in the habit of passing out free money, he tried to balance it as best he could.

Once a month, Dad dropped in for a haircut from his favorite hairdresser— Keller. Keller would have a vodka and soda ready for Dad. They discussed business, and Keller learned of any problems that needed a trim. One of them was a beer distributor named Sam Dunagan. I don't know what problems he had with Big T, but he just disappeared one day. My guess was it involved a loan default and got resolved. Justice looked different in my household.

While all this was going on, I managed to make the National Honor Society in high school. I would eventually graduate with honors, receiving a second-place award for an essay on Kennedy's inauguration speech. These accomplishments kept Dad off my ass—mostly.

As for my flying career, I began hanging out at Meacham Field in northwest Fort Worth. Dad had moved his Cessna there and added a Comanche 250. The Comanche was a single-engine low-wing aircraft, with four seats and retractable landing gear. It could haul more than the Cessna. It was a solid plane.

When I turned seventeen, I was able to get my private license. This allowed me to fly passengers, but not for money. Big T didn't care. One day, he pulled me aside. "Son, I want you to fly down to Mexia and pick up some wetbacks. The factories up here need them. Cram as many as you can in the Aero Commander, even if it means tossing some gear or going light. Land at the Grand Prairie Airport only. Do you understand?"

"But the Aero Commander has two engines," I said. "You know I can't legally fly it until I'm eighteen *and* I have a commercial, multi-engine, instrument license."

"Son, we're robbing a bank and you're worried that the insurance card is missing from the glove compartment? Stop overthinking this. Understand?"

I understood. Dad pulled out a map and showed me how to do it without getting caught.

My first trip was going to be nerve-wracking no matter how much I prepared. The Aero Commander—Dad's third plane—was a twin engine that could legally hold six passengers. By "going light," which meant carrying less fuel, I could squeeze in two more passengers who would have to sit on the floor. Having less fuel shouldn't be a problem since Mexia was two hours southeast of Fort Worth by car. If I ran out, there were plenty of airstrips to land at. Of course, I'd have to let my passengers out at the end of the runway so they could run for the hills. It would be bad enough without a proper license. But carrying passengers *and* being above the rated passenger limit? That would put me in jail.

Like Dad told me, I logged a flight plan with the FAA and took off. When I neared Mexia, at the very last moment, I deviated from the flight plan. Spotting a particular barn, I flew low, buzzing it. This was a signal for the men inside to load up the illegal aliens—I mean undocumented workers—and drive them to the airport. By the time I landed and came to a stop, the van was just pulling up. We hardly exchanged words as eight nervous and scared Mexicans crammed themselves into a space designed for six. As the ground crew slammed the door shut, I revved up the engines and took off, minutes before the FAA inspectors could arrive.

When I landed in Grand Prairie, a van was there to take the passengers and turn them into *documented* workers. Then they went to a factory where they punched in and worked a twelve-hour shift. It was a real tight operation, engineered well by Big T and overseen by Marilyn Crenshaw.

I made this run several times over a period of months. Each time, I worried about getting caught. Thankfully, I never did.

In the spring of 1970, I turned eighteen and received my commercial license and flight instructor license. Now, I could get paid for hauling passengers and teaching folks how to fly. It was a gift from heaven.

Dad had me flying one of his planes from Meacham to Mangham a lot because he didn't like driving the extra mileage to Meacham. That was fine with me. The more hours I logged, the closer I got to my next accomplishment: a multi-engine license. Wherever his planes were, I was usually close by.

I continued hanging out at either Mangham or Meacham. If people showed up looking to fly, I had a chance of convincing them that I was the right guy. If I wasn't teaching classes, I was sweeping the hangar, washing planes—anything for money. Money bought gas. And planes drink gas.

Being eighteen meant graduation was near. I graduated from Richland High School with honors. My father gave me a blue Camaro Z28 as a graduation gift. The racing stripes made this car look faster, although it was already pretty fast.

Our prom was held as a graduation party dance. My date, Cynthia Lever, was thoroughly impressed with my new car. We looked good driving up to the hotel and tossing the keys to the valet. However, she had a little bit too much to drink at the dance. I was forced to carry her out to the car, holding her over my shoulder while I searched for the valet ticket with my spare hand. I drove her home as fast as that Z28 could go. No way was she throwing up all over my leather seats and ruining that new car smell. Fortunately, we made it to her home. I carried her inside, putting her on the couch and straightening her dress so she looked like a lady. I never saw her again, mainly because

I had one simple rule: If you get drunk and pass out on me, no more dates. It was something I tried to live by.

One of Dad's crew—Cliff Eisenman—ran a furniture store. I was working at the Western Hills Inn one Monday when Dad and Keller rushed out and raced to the furniture store. Later, I learned what that was all about.

Cliff's store had been raided by the FBI. Apparently, he'd done something shady like launder money. He would sell a couch for $50 but log $250 as income. Then he would deposit $200 in illegal money into the bank. After he paid taxes on it, the money was clean. I believed that some of the money came from Big T's gambling and bookmaking operations and was run through that store. This went on for years.

When Keller Colton got involved, it was usually a serious matter. Sure enough, Cliff was there one day and gone the next. All I heard was that he was in the witness protection program. It was very hush-hush. Who was being protected, though, I had no idea.

After this, Dad let me see his operation at the Great Southwest Golf Club. It was a men's only golf club, and one of the best courses in Texas. Because it was strictly for men, there was a small clubhouse— no swimming pools or tennis courts. Big T had a gambling operation set up in the rear locker room. It was full of poker tables. Tough guys restricted the access so Big T could control it. Unlike Western Hills Inn, gambling at this place operated only during daytime hours.

The gambling would start in the morning. Sometimes they'd get up from the tables, play a round of golf, and then come back to gamble some more. They mostly played poker with a rake to Big T and other table sponsors.

When he started this operation, Big T used money. But somehow, a couple of members who didn't gamble said something to someone. Word got out. Dad and the Grand Prairie mayor were very close. He told Dad to change to redeemable chips. Big T did, and the gambling continued.

The Great Southwest Golf Club was very private. Lots of celebrities played there, including the singer B.J. Thomas. Professional golfers like Ben Crenshaw and Chi-Chi Rodriguez played there too. I played in the PGA Colonial NIT Pro-Am Golf Tournament and scored a hole in one. That made the papers. The poker tables didn't.

One day, I had played a round of golf and came in to watch this gin rummy player clean out a few guys. Studying his tactics, I knew I could take him. My card-playing skills were good, usually relieving cash from my friends' wallets.

"Mind if I sit down?" I asked the player.

"Be my guest," he said politely.

We fired up the cards and went at it. When we were done, his winnings added up to $500. In 1970, that was a lot of money.

I glanced at my opponent and saw him grin. Unfortunately, there was nothing I could do about it because I had lost to him. I was busy trying hard to figure a way to pay him when a man pulled the player aside. I could barely hear the whispered conversation.

"Hey, do you know who you just beat?"

"No," the player said. "Who?"

"That's Big T's son."

"Oh shit!" the player said, rubbing his jaw.

"I suggest you give the money back."

The player stood there for a few minutes before turning back to me. "Uhh, listen up, son. You shouldn't be playing with all these skilled sharks around here. I'm going to erase your debt. And let that be a lesson to you!" he said, adding emphasis on the last part.

It was a definitely a lesson—a very valuable one. Never again did I sit down and play cards for money.

The gambling operation was very profitable. Big T also made money by making loans out of both gambling locations. I say Big T, but I really mean his men. Big T didn't physically handle the money or deal with anything at the lower levels. He sat at the top giving orders when necessary and Marilyn Crenshaw ensured they were carried out.

At the golf course, one man—an ex-NFL stud—lost a great deal of money at the card tables. Whether he needed the money for gambling or something else, I didn't know. However, he was soon invited to leave the state of Texas subject to paying the money back. And leave he did. I'm not sure he ever returned but he did become an NFL coach in another city.

Marilyn Crenshaw continued running Dad's operations. She stayed mostly clear of me, which was fine. I didn't want to see her.

One day, I had this hot girlfriend in my Z28 and was paying close attention to her. Instantly, traffic stopped. If I had been looking, I would have seen it. Instead, I rear-ended the car in front of me, totaling my new ride. When the driver got out, I saw he was an angry Mexican. The cops were called and I had to listen while he told his story and threatened to sue me. Next thing I knew, Big T rolled into action. And just like that, the problem went away.

What also disappeared were the brand new Z28 *and* the hot chick. In their place was a beat-up tan Ford Pinto and an empty passenger's seat. Marilyn Crenshaw had given me her old car. It was a terrible piece of junk, but at least it ran. I couldn't believe I was going to have to drive it to the University of Texas. Yet Big T was adamant. I had to admit, the man understood justice.

Chapter Four

N ow that I was out of high school, it was time to plan for my future. I was registered to attend the University of Texas in the fall, where I hoped to play football. I sent my films to Darrell Royal, the head coach, who had just finished celebrating the Longhorns' 1969 national championship. I wanted to play there so I could help them go back-to-back. But Coach Royal turned me down, said I was too small. "Son, you're only six feet tall." By then, they were putting out these big huge monsters who rammed into each other. I wasn't one of them.

Undeterred, I sent my films to Ohio State. After seeing my best stuff, Woody Hayes called me in for an interview. I grabbed Dad's Comanche and flew up there alone. After shaking my hand, Hayes gave me the up-down and echoed Coach Royal: "Son, you're too small."

These two men were at the top of their profession. I figured they had to know what they were doing. That pushed me toward my other option: the Air Force Academy.

Because I wanted to be a pilot for a big airline, I thought the only way was through the military. I would have to join the service and learn through them or attend a military academy. But you don't just walk into a military academy. You need a recommendation from your congressman.

Dad wanted me to be a doctor. That was his plan for my life. When I talked to him about joining a military academy, I couched it with phrases like, "Med school is expensive. I can learn on their dime." At the time, boys were being drafted for Vietnam. A lot of those boys came back in caskets. With six to eight years in med school, my dad assumed the war would be over and I would be the coveted doctor.

Dad put his network to the test and made some inquiries. His connections worked well selling government surplus non-FAA-approved parts, hardware, minks, and boats. He even had politicians dropping some cash in his illegal gambling operation. But amazingly, those same politicians didn't want to help the son of some aircraft parts and lighting vendor get into the military. It was a possible "conflict of interest," they said. Sure. Now that I'm older, I get it.

Out of options, I was left to attend the University of Texas, which wasn't a bad deal. I spent the summer hanging out at Meacham Field, making extra money by giving flying lessons and picking up nonpaying flights to add hours to my logbook. Oh, and I made plenty of runs down to Mexia, bringing back the endless stream of illegals hungry for good-paying factory jobs. I also ran errands for Big T, making sure his cash pipeline continued flowing in the right direction.

As for vehicles, I drove Marilyn Crenshaw's Pinto and hated every minute of it. I kept thinking Dad would replace it with a better vehicle. Most parents would have, but he didn't. It taught me a valuable lesson.

In the fall of 1970, I drove to Austin and located my dorm. Stepping out of that ugly Pinto was a well-dressed boy from Fort Worth. I imagined the other boys laughing at me while the girls kept their distance. What I didn't count on was a lack of on-campus parking. I was able to hide my Pinto on some distant lot, keeping it well out of sight. This allowed me to join the Pi Kappa Alpha fraternity and get down to what I really wanted to do: party.

During football season, our team was good again. Coach Royal somehow won back-to-back national championships without my help. And that meant more parties to celebrate. In fact, if they gave a grade for having a good time, I would have received an A. Unfortunately, they didn't. I earned high Cs in my first year—extremely low marks for me. When Dad saw them, he was very disappointed.

I arrived back home for the summer to an unhappy father. He made sure I was completely partied out by working me hard. I had to clean toilets and deliver room service to the gamblers on the B-Wing. During breaks, I managed to hang out again at Meacham Field, dreaming of flying.

One day, Dad came into the Caribe Club and pulled me aside. "Tom, I need to fly to Los Angeles. Our West Coast rep lives there and has some lighting designs I need to review. It's hard for me to fly by myself. I need you to come and spell me at the controls."

Let's see… stay here and clean toilets, or get back in a plane? He didn't have to tell me twice.

We flew the larger Aero Commander, taking turns at the controls. When we landed safely, we drove to the rep's house so Dad could get to work. I napped on the couch, watching television and relaxing.

Around six, the rep suggested we all go out to dinner. He had called a babysitter to watch his kids, whom his wife had kept away from the house. Now that they were back, I could see they were too young to leave alone.

I was dusting myself off and straightening my clothes when the doorbell rang. With no one answering it, I jumped into action. As I swung the door open, I had to blink several times. The babysitter's name was Cindy Ogden and she was painfully cute. "Come right in," I said. "You must be the babysitter."

"If you're one of the kids I'm watching, this should be fun."

"If you close your eyes, I could be," I said, laughing. When she laughed, there was an instant connection.

During dinner, I kept thinking about her. When we returned, not sure if I'd ever see her again, I asked her out. She agreed. I saw her the next night before we took off back to Fort Worth.

In the air, I saw her face in every cloud. When we landed, I devoted every waking moment to earning gas money or scrounging it up any way I could. I took the cheaper single-engine Comanche to Los Angeles many times during that summer. I certainly added a ton of hours to my logbook.

During those trips, I had a lot of time in the air to think. How could Cindy and I spend more time together? It was during a visit to a local L.A. bar—when they were giving away Hawaiian leis— that I hatched a plot to see Cindy more. I just needed to find the right time to ask Dad.

At the end of each quarter, Dad received his commission check from Grimes. With his check in hand, I knew he'd be one happy man. When that same moment dovetailed with a large haul from a weekend's worth of gambling, he was one giddy mafia don. Seeing him flush with cash, I decided to make my move.

"Dad, I'd like to attend the University of Hawaii."

"What?" he asked, the smile disappearing from his face.

"Yeah, you know, I really liked it when I was out there. I'd like to go back. Maybe even graduate from there."

He shook his head in disbelief. "All I remember is that scare we had. Your mother and I thought you were a goner."

The scare he was talking about happened during the summer between my junior and senior year. I was attending a school in Hawaii. Swope International put together summer classes for high school students to take at far-off locations. This allowed rich kids like me to experience an exotic place while clearing away courses like physics and calculus for my senior year. Dad knew about this company because he had a connection in Beaumont, Texas, where Swope International was located. The man told him it was a good idea to send me there because I'd likely get As while experiencing life away from the parents. "Prepare him for college, for being on his own," the man said, selling Dad on the cost. Yet Dad had a different motivation. He wanted me to have an easy final year—one I could make straight As—so I'd graduate with honors. This was important to his carefully laid-out plan of me becoming a doctor.

The company's school was located on the island of Kauai. It's the garden island of Hawaii, full of waterfalls and tropical jungles. I had my private pilot's license, so Dad knew I was renting a Cessna and flying around the islands. There was no telephone service to or from the island, which left us to communicate by mail or ham radio.

One day, Mom opened the paper and read about a young boy from Fort Worth who had been killed flying his plane in Kauai. Dad spent all day working a ham radio to reach Kauai. Finally, he reached my school, who told him I was fine. Against all odds, it was some *other* boy from Fort Worth who'd been killed flying a Cessna. That incident had left my parents with some bad feelings. Now, two years later, I was dredging them back up.

"What about becoming a doctor?" Dad asked, his eyebrows forming a deep V. "How can you study medicine out there?"

"I've been thinking about that," I said, preparing him for the big pitch. "With all the advanced work on mining the oceans, I've decided I want to be an oceanographer."

This caught him off guard, making him pause. At the time, the ocean was big news. Jacques Cousteau was a star, along with other TV shows involving dolphins and sea life like *Voyage to the Bottom of the Sea*, *Sea Hunt*, and *Flipper*. Oceanography was the new and sexy profession.

"Oceanography," he said, his eyes shifting up. "Huh."

With this response, I could tell he was buying what I was selling. It was time to push the accelerator to the floor. "Yeah, just think—a Toler as an oceanographer. I'll be out there protecting the reefs, setting up sea farms, and even creating new colonies under the ocean. They say we'll be searching for wrecked ships while we're out there. Maybe even find buried treasure."

He pursed his lips at the thought of buried treasure. I could see him imagining a gold doubloon hanging around his neck. "Son, let me think about it. I'll let you know."

I knew it was a done deal. In fact, I applied to the University of Hawaii the next day and called Cindy to tell her I was going. She was hitting up her father with the same plan, but her pitch was easier since a lot of rich kids from Los Angeles went to school in Hawaii.

Over the next week, we made our plans while I waited for an answer. When Dad finally said yes, I was extremely happy. My new girlfriend and I would be together in paradise, with our parents footing the bill. I could hardly wait.

I arrived in Hawaii a week early, getting settled in my room and meeting my new dormmates. I shopped around and quickly located a light blue Ford Mustang for sale, buying it on the spot. This Mustang was perfect for cruising the island with the top down. Now, all I needed was Cindy sitting next to me and a video camera mounted on its hood and I'd have my own TV show. It was perfect.

Until it wasn't.

Right before school started, I received a Dear Tom letter from Cindy. According to the letter I burned, she had fallen in love with someone else who was taller and better looking than me. Thus, she was staying in Los Angeles where he attended college. As the paper turned to ashes, I thought about this new development. She wasn't clear, but I wanted to believe she had met this guy in the last two days. I didn't want to think she had let me go through all this knowing she'd have to dump me when I arrived in Hawaii. No one could be that cruel. Right?

I leaned back in my chair and studied the ugly gray paint of my dorm wall. The only reason I was in Hawaii was to be with Cindy. I didn't know anyone, nor did I want to be here. And I had to start learning about plankton, sea anemone, and the layers of earth going down to the core. Man, I liked flying *over* that crap, not studying it. Oh, the unfairness of it all! The only good news was that my grades came up.

One day, I was bored and decided to check out the Departure Lounge. It was a classy disco in the Americana Hawaiian Hotel. It usually had good live music.

As I took a seat at a table near the band, I noticed the female drummer. She was hot. It didn't take long to forget Cindy and fall in love with Vicki McIntyre. We quickly became inseparable.

As an added bonus, her father, an American Airlines captain flying the Pacific, told me how I could be an airline pilot without having to go through the military. He pointed to his son, Mike, who was a very young hire right out of an aviation program somewhere up north. I called my dad and told him I wanted to join that aviation program after finishing up my sophomore year. He had gone from having a doctor for a son to an oceanographer. Now, the truth had finally made an appearance.

"Son, I'm flying out there so we can discuss this." This translated to, "So I can talk you out of this nonsense."

The aviation program Mike took was the… I wish I could remember it.

"It was Purdue University Aviation School," Vicki clarified. "And it was the Ala Moana Hotel, not the Americana Hawaiian Hotel. The Departure Lounge was in the Ala Moana. Come on, Tom, are you getting old on me?"

I turned to my left and saw Vicki McIntyre sitting in what should be an empty first mate's chair. "How did you get in my wheelhouse?" I asked, not believing my eyes. "Only two people boarded this boat and you weren't one of them!"

"That's true," she said. "But you didn't think I'd let you screw up all these details on your own, did you? Besides, I had to see this dog you're so proud of. Duke—is that your name?"

Duke sauntered over, sniffed her hand, and started licking it.

"I guess I'm good people," she said. "So, how have you been, Tom? It's been a few years."

I blinked several times, still in disbelief. Yet there she was, my old girlfriend. And just like she looked in 1971. She didn't even flinch as another wave crashed against the boat, sending me scrambling to readjust things.

"Vicki, I've thought of you often," I said as the ocean calmed for a moment. "What a time we had in Hawaii. And I sure owe your dad. That night we sat at the table and he told me how I could become a pilot for the airlines changed my life."

She smiled. "I'm glad he could help. He had a good career at American Airlines. He may have saved your life."

"What are you talking about?"

"Remember how many soldiers on R&R from Vietnam came into that disco while we played? They'd come back five months later and say the two buddies who were with them last time got it in some rice field or stepped on a land mine. I didn't want that for you. I knew you wanted to be a pilot so bad you would've gone into the service. When Dad called and said he was on a layover, I just had to make sure he met you and told you there was another way."

"Well, I had a great career at American Airlines. I know you eventually signed up with United Airlines. How long were you with them?"

"Thirty-four years. I did the flight attendant thing along with emergency training, chief purser of international flights, and some video training. I even got to play the drums for United."

"That's fantastic," I said. "Where do you live now?"

"Las Vegas."

"How are your parents?" I asked.

Her face darkened as she paused. After a few seconds, she replied in a low voice. "They're long gone."

"Oh, I'm so sorry." I turned the wheel to avoid a large wave. "Wally had a big impact on my life. They had an impact on you too, right? You were adopted, if I remember correctly."

"You're right. My brother, Mike, and I were unrelated—just two kids four years apart at some agency in Kansas City. One day, Mom and Dad plucked us out and drove us to our forever home. They took such great care of us that when it was their time to go, I moved them out to Las Vegas and put them in my house. I was so grateful to take care of them to their dying breaths. It was the highlight of my life."

"That's wonderful. And Mike? I remember he was hired by Playboy to fly their DC-9. That had to be a dream job. What's he doing now?"

"Married and retired. He lives in Puerto Vallarta half the time and Vancouver the other half. I'll let you figure out which half. He even plays guitar in bands at both places."

"You and Mike were always music makers. I still remember when I first saw you playing the drums. Oh wow!"

She laughed. "Me?! What about you? After I finished that set, I came over to your table to say hi, hoping you'd buy me a drink. All I saw was this tall, tan, blond-haired Adonis dressed super sharp. When you flashed that big smile, I was done. It was instant love."

"I wish I had that body now." I glanced down at my weathered hands, dotted with age spots. "I'm trying to stay alert so we can reach land. Duke here has been keeping me awake, nipping on my shoe."

"I can see that," Vicki said. "Judging from the piece that's missing, I guess he's been doing his job."

"He has. Say, what happened to us?"

"You remember—I got sick and went back to Chicago. After nine months in Hawaii, you returned to Fort Worth and completed your college degree. Then you made your career as an airline pilot." She sat there staring at me, grinning. "I can't tell you how many times in those thirty-four years I got off the plane and looked for that tall, handsome Texan. I often wondered if I'd imagined our relationship."

"No, you didn't imagine it." I peered over at her, mustering up a crooked smile. "Did you marry?"

"I did. We had a daughter, Kristen, who's the pride and blessing of my life. My husband passed in 2007. Did you ever have kids?"

"No. All I had is this wonderful dog, Duke. When I look back over my life—the family, the women—he's all I have now. Isn't that right, Duke?"

I looked down at my dog, who stood dutifully, watching my every move. "You know, Vicki, I never told you…" I glanced at the first mate's chair to meet her eyes, but she was gone. "Vicki? Where are you?"

I closed my eyes and opened them again. All I saw were the white tips of the endless waves I needed to navigate. I shook my head several times to clear the cobwebs, but still didn't see that cute young drummer who'd stolen my heart.

With a sigh, I gazed up at the sky. That's when I noticed the stars were visible. Using my Coast Guard training, I looked for the North Star and couldn't find it. The second choice was Venus. I spotted that ahead. If I could keep it in the windshield, I'd be heading in the right direction.

Another wave splashed over us. Vicki was gone, but the ocean wasn't.

"Duke, it's time to get back to work."

Chapter Five

After my year in Hawaii, I landed back in Fort Worth only to be greeted by Big T. He hugged me, then fished out a list of things to do from his pocket and handed it to me. It was the usual: cleaning toilets, busboy work, and maintaining his airplanes. But I had my own plan. While he worked me, I was working him over. Eventually, he saw that I was fiercely determined to be a pilot and gave in. Together, we came up with a plan that could work for the both of us.

First, I had to get that all-important commercial multi-engine instrument rating. I looked for available flight schools and sat down with Dad to go over my list. One of them was near Dad's company, Grimes Manufacturing, in Urbana, Ohio. He made some calls and all of a sudden, I was headed to Urbana.

An executive with Grimes had an apartment nearby. He let me stay in a spare bedroom for free while I attended a flight school in Dayton. The school had a twin-engine Piper that held six passengers. This was the perfect setup to get my multi-engine license.

As an added bonus, Grimes had three Beech 18s. Their mission was to fly Grimes's executives to clients' factories all over the U.S. Even though these planes didn't require a copilot, through Dad's connections, I was able to be the copilot *and* log valuable flight time because the corporate pilots were certified instructors. Sure, I wasn't getting paid to fly, but I didn't care. I needed the hours.

After a few weeks, the Grimes pilots saw my experience. They moved me to the left seat, which helped log hours faster. Plus, I was actually flying the plane. When I wasn't flying for Grimes, I was at the flight school working toward my license. With Dad paying for everything, it was a fun time.

I spent the summer up there learning and flying. When I was done, I had my commercial multi-engine rating. This allowed me to fly anything for pay except scheduled operations like the national airlines, UPS, and FedEx. If it was nonscheduled—which most charter and corporate flights are—I could fly it. Now, I hoped to make some good money. Unfortunately, all I could find back in Fort Worth was giving flying lessons. I was undeterred.

When fall rolled around, I needed to complete my final two years in college. Going to the University of Texas was out. Too much partying there. And Hawaii was off the menu now that my oceanographer cover had been blown. That left the University of Texas at Arlington. UTA is a good-sized college located right next to Grand Prairie. It has all the disciplines of bigger colleges, and it's part of the University of Texas system. This gives it some cachet. But the big plus for me was that I could keep hanging around the local airports like Meacham before and after class, hoping to pick up some paying pilot work.

As time went by, Big T and Mom accepted my new career path. Even my younger brother, Gary, was taking up flying. And why not? Big T was in the aircraft lighting business. He could hand over a huge book of *legitimate* business to one of us when and if he retired. The whole thing made sense. And thank God I could stop pretending I wanted to be a doctor or oceanographer. No more blood or dissecting fish for me.

During my last two years in college, I made money giving flying lessons to whoever walked up. If there were charter flights going out, I tried to hitch a ride as a copilot to add hours to my logbook. Those flights didn't pay, but I didn't care. I was still living with my parents, so my overhead was low.

One outfit I hooked on with was a travel club. Back then, you couldn't run an airline regularly flying people around without a serious infrastructure and inspections by the FAA. This was so expensive that only the corporations who ran professional airlines could swing the costs. The other option was to buy your own plane. That way, you could take off when and where you wanted. However, one person and even one company might not be able to shoulder such a large cost as the plane, hangar space, pilots, insurance, and maintenance. Wouldn't it be nice if lots of people could get together and help fund a plane? Enter the Sportsman's Air Travel Club.

Two men out of Meacham Field purchased three DC-3 passenger planes, formerly owned by Eastern Airlines. Owning and maintaining these large planes was expensive. That's why the clientele of Sportsman's was upscale. Think rich folks—executives, celebrities, business owners, and trust fund babies. Sportsman's had regularly scheduled trips to Mexico for hunting and fishing, usually leaving Thursday. You couldn't fly on the plane unless you were a member of the club and paid regular dues. The owners claimed they weren't selling air travel, just vacation packages. The air travel just happened to be a small part of the package. Add in the fact that most passengers paid cash for the trips, and it was easy for them to fly under the FAA's radar.

I began schmoozing with the owners of these DC-3s. Under FAA rules, a DC-3 weighed enough to require a copilot. This meant the owners had to shell out money for a second person. That's where I saw an angle.

I talked to them about letting me be the copilot. I proposed a deal: So long as they covered lodging and meals, I would work for free. Eventually, they agreed. This deal allowed me to add hours to my logbook while experiencing all the wild adventures that came with it.

Because I was still in school and the trips lasted four days, I would miss class on Thursdays and Fridays. I had to take my books with me to study in the hotel.

We usually flew to El Fuerte, a small town in Mexico forty miles inland from the Gulf of California. All around were small lakes— ideal for largemouth bass and dove hunting. There were several camps that catered to rich Americans. I never went to the camps, staying only in the city. That was where the fun started.

The groups we carried were all men, many of whom started drinking the second they stepped onto the plane. For the next five-plus hours, they ate and drank, and not necessarily in that order. When we landed, one of my duties as copilot kicked in.

With the plane parked and the engines off, I eased myself under the belly, back to the tail section near the rear wheel. There, I located the trapdoor. Undoing the fasteners, I stepped away as the trapdoor swung down. Right above it was the honey pot. This was the receptacle that held all the waste from the toilet inside the plane. The toilet had no running water; it was just a simple pot. This meant it was all waste and no added filler like flushed water.

These planes didn't have suction hose holes to take everything out. Instead, someone had to carefully balance the large bucket with one hand while slowly turning the Dzus fasteners away from the lip with the other hand. This was hard to do with one person. Really, you needed someone holding the bucket while another person turned the fasteners. Yet the space was cramped. Fitting two people in was next to impossible. And, if you weren't careful, you might get covered in "honey."

After the first trip to El Fuerte, I discovered that for a few U.S. dollars, a local Mexican would empty it for me. Sure, I wasn't getting paid to make this trip. But for two dollars, it was worth it for someone else to risk splashing themselves. The only problem with my strategy was the passengers. These men loaded that honey pot up each trip. It was heavy and full, almost to the brim of the toilet. Thus, the local Mexicans continually raised the price on me. I didn't blame them. These crazy rich guys' bodies sure could process the food and booze.

One day, I arrived in El Fuerte, stretched out my arms in the gorgeous sunshine of Mexico, and walked down the stairs to the waiting Mexicans, only to discover the price to change the honey pot was now twenty dollars. In the early 1970s, that was a lot of money—too much for me to pay. Unwilling to part with a Jackson, I was forced to do it myself. Trust me, it was nasty work.

I soon began to dread the smells of used beer, whiskey, and sausage. I hoped that over time, the free market of El Fuerte would bring down the price to ten bucks or less. Sadly, it did not. The local Mexicans did not need U.S. dollars bad enough to slop a large container of human waste three hundred yards to the airport dump.

If I thought the trip to Mexico was bad, coming back home was the worst. For three days, these men crammed so much booze and Mexican food into their bodies, something had to give. That "give" occurred on the return trip home. Between throwing up and a dozen sit-downs, the toilet threatened to spill with each slight dip of the wings. By the time we landed, I was willing to pay $100 for someone to change out the honey pot. Thankfully, Ernie was there.

Ernie was a line boy, someone who did everything—sweeping the hangar, pushing a plane out, cleaning, you name it. And Ernie liked to make extra cash. Ten bucks was enough for him to handle the honey pot; that is, until one rather rough trip back. We had taken two extra passengers and they were big ol' boys. I was frightened to see what might come out of their three-days-in-Mexico intestines.

Like always, Ernie met me at the plane. I told him I had his ten bucks in my right front pocket. "Come find me in the lounge when you have it cleaned."

He nodded as he crouched under the plane's belly and located the trap door. Opening that up, he positioned himself to put his left hand in the center. Then he took the screwdriver in his right hand to begin twisting the fasteners. I was going to hide in the lounge but thought it might be wise to stick around in case he needed help. Before I could put a piece of chewing gum in my mouth, I heard a noise and saw the bucket come loose, sloshing Ernie on the way down. Its base hit the tarmac with authority, sending a cascade of El Fuerte fun back into poor Ernie's face, neck, and back. He started dancing around, wailing and swatting at the mess like it was a band of angry hornets. I lifted my handheld radio and pressed the send button. "Tower Chief, come in."

"This is the Tower Chief, over."

"Is that you, Bob?" I asked.

"Yeah, Tom. You just get back?"

"Yeah. I'm on that DC-3 down there. Listen, I got an emergency. My line boy just got hit in the face with a pot of poop. Honey bucket fell on him."

"Do you want me to roll the CFR?" he said nonchalantly. CFR was the Crash Fire Rescue.

"One truck'll be fine."

A minute later, the fire truck arrived and hosed Ernie down. It was a real mess. But I still gave him his ten bucks. Incredibly, he didn't raise the price on me the next time. Ernie wasn't the brightest, but he sure was my hero.

After several trips to Mexico, I got to know some of the regulars. Two of them were brothers—Billy and Willy Wortham—who owned a construction company in Fort Worth. They built office buildings and hotels, apparently making a lot of money. How they both got nicknames from the singular formal name of William, I had no idea.

Next to them was Paul Pennington, a developer who hired the Worthams to build his projects. They seemed cozy with each other. The other regular was Marcel Rivers. Marcel was a plastic surgeon in Dallas, rolling in dough. During one drunken encounter, Marcel explained that his real name was Mark, but the women like being examined by a guy named Marcel.

Mixed in with these guys were bankers, lawyers, car dealers, and all sorts of characters. The important motivation of these trips was giving these men a chance to let their hair down. Away from the missus, they could eat and drink everything, tell crude jokes, pee anywhere they liked, and fire off guns at will. It was a miracle someone didn't get their head blown off.

After we landed in El Fuerte, the pilots and I cleaned up and readied the plane. Then we went to town where we checked into a hotel until it was time to go. Thus, we were separated from these guys most of the time. Occasionally, though, there was some reason to be with them. One of those occasions happened in June, when we were leaving Mexico and heading back home.

I was in the copilot's seat on the right side. Like usual, we taxied to the end of the runway—nothing more than a hard-packed grass strip—and revved up the engines. Once the engines reached capacity, the pilot pushed the throttle forward and we began rolling down the runway. Just as our wheels departed the dirt, a jug on my side blew. A jug is a cylinder in the engine, also called a piston. This is extremely dangerous, because your right engine becomes almost useless. We could have crashed right there.

Without enough engine power to reach a high altitude, we weren't going to make it back to Fort Worth. Landing back on the grass strip wasn't an option, because there would be no way to fix the aircraft. Instead, we headed to a commercial airport in Los Mochis, a large city on the coast, and landed there. But our problems had just begun.

First, we had no one paid off in Los Mochis. This is critical in Mexico. When the local authority came to inspect our plane, they found guns and ammunition. Most developing countries don't like their citizens to have guns, because they can be used to shoot the leaders. And it's easier to keep control of the population when all they can do is throw rocks at you.

The second issue we had was spare parts. We happened to be carrying a spare jug, which made them upset. The game they liked to play was to sell you their parts at highly inflated prices. It was like the mafia, where a $10 part was marked up to $150 so everyone could get a piece. I could relate.

To solve these problems, we were going to have to spread around a lot of cash. That would leave us with nothing to pay the mechanics to take apart the engine and install the jug. Fortunately, one of the owners of the travel club knew the governor of the state of Sinaloa, where we had landed. That got us a free pass. Now all we had to do was find and pay the local Mexican labor to install the jug. Enter new problems.

Billy and Willy, the crazy building contractors, whipped up the already-drunk passengers into a frenzy. Out of nowhere, or at least an empty Tequila bottle, they wanted to go to Boy's Town and check out the women. Dr. Rivers agreed, saying it would be an excellent opportunity to inspect the local breasts. When the owner of the travel club acquiesced, transportation was quickly arranged and off we went.

Boy's Town was pretty rustic, basically a good place to get mugged with your pants down. Billy and Willy, along with Doc Rivers and Paul Pennington, wanted to take their girls back to the local town—mainly the hotel we were supposed to stay at. The bartenders of the taverns where these girls worked wouldn't allow their girls to leave. After all, they may never come back. There was no way they were letting their cash cows out of the barn. This created a Mexican standoff.

Billy and Willy weren't ones to sit down and throw up their hands at the first roadblock. They'd made millions by overcoming obstacles. After sizing up the situation, they threw their fists into the bartenders' faces. With the bartenders out of commission, the girls were free to come with us.

Taxis pulled up and took our group to the hotel. There, we found the policía waiting for us. Since they had guns and ours were back on the plane, they removed the girls from our possession and escorted us to the local jail. Our fun had just begun.

At the jail, they removed our watches, rings, money—everything of value. I was concerned mainly because they snagged my last ten bucks. This was money for Ernie and my honey pot dump. When I got inside the jail, though, I forgot all about the honey pot and my confiscated ten dollars.

The jail was like something out of medieval times. That's when it was probably built. A hole in the corner allowed you to stand over it and drop whatever waste you had, so long as you hit the hole. If you missed—well, the dirt floor doubled as a bed. Good luck with that.

I was in a cell with Doc Rivers and a bunch of drunk Mexicans. They had staked out the floor away from the hole, so the Doc and I had to get close to it. We did get to see a rat coming in to inspect the latest leavings. That was interesting.

With no one but me to talk to, the good doctor provided details about his profession. He said he'd probably examined most of the breasts in Dallas. Breasts were his bread and butter. He also performed work on faces, but didn't handle much else. If he did his job properly, he'd leave no fingerprints for the guy who came after him.

Listening to him, I briefly reconsidered the medical profession. But then I remembered the blood and nixed that idea. I told him I'd just have to be satisfied with becoming a pilot.

"Son," he said, putting his hand on my shoulder, "I'm pretty sure a good-looking pilot in a nice uniform can see lots of my handiwork *without* having to go to med school."

I began wondering if he was a real doctor.

After he ran out of stories, I was ready to leave. Once again, a call to the same governor freed us from this hellhole. And the policía kindly reached into their pockets—otherwise known as a Mexican evidence locker—and returned our money and valuables. We took taxis back to the hotel, where we remained until the plane was repaired.

Normally, a good mechanic could change out a jug in three to four hours. These Mexicans took a full day. The next afternoon, we boarded the plane, closed the door, and were thankful when the wheels came up and the plane headed for home.

Besides taking the travel club to Mexico, the owners of the DC-3s rented them out for other events. One of them was the National Parachute Championships held in Tahlequah, Oklahoma. Parachutists there were trying to set a record by having twenty-five people hold hands in the shape of a star. At the time, the record was twenty-two.

The reason they needed a DC-3, especially one that was cargo configured, was the big doors. These allowed more people to jump out at once, which increased the chances of everyone linking up.

The group organizing this three-day event chartered two of the club's DC-3s and two Beech 18s. That meant a lot of pilots and copilots were needed. When I threw up my hand, I was selected for duty in one of the DC-3s. On this trip, I would be the actual copilot.

Even though there were four different planes there, our DC-3 was selected for the big stunt. One plane was all that was needed, because it was too dangerous to have people jumping from multiple planes. A lot of bad things could happen. The planes could touch, since they'd have to be close to each other. That would likely mean crashing. If one plane was above the other, the jumpers might hit the wing of the plane below or, God forbid, the propellers. There had already been one disaster. During a preliminary contest, the other DC-3 had gone up to let some guys practice jumping. I'd been on the ground, standing next to a cute girl who wanted to teach me how to pack a parachute. I really didn't care how to pack a chute, so long as I could stand next to her. While I was learning, the DC-3 worked its way up to 12,000 feet. When one of the men jumped out, his chute became tangled. The proper procedure is to pull the ring tab on each shoulder, releasing the main chute. Once that is clear, the skydiver pulls the backup chute. Hopefully this doesn't get tangled.

When we saw everyone looking up at the sky, we followed their gazes and spotted the jumper with the tangled chute. Unfortunately, he had not released his main chute—something any jumper is hesitant to do. He pulled his reserve chute and it got tangled up in his main chute, neither of which slowed him down. He hit the ground so hard we had to dig him out. I thought the whole thing would be canceled, but skydivers are tough. They held a moment of silence and the event continued, unaltered.

55

On the day of the record-setting jump, I sat through the preflight briefings, studying my notes. To give the jumpers enough time to link up and set the record, we needed to climb to 12,000 feet. The higher a plane goes, the thinner the air. The DC-3 could handle it, but it would take some time to get that high. It also meant more fuel, adding to the already heavy load of twenty-five jumpers.

When we had the plane ready, twenty-five jumpers piled in. I was about to close the door when five more jumpers pushed their way on. They were the judges and cameramen. This was more than we'd been told, making us way overweight. I would've ordered someone to get out, but the pilot decided to try it. Worst-case scenario we would crash and experience a fiery death.

The airfield we were using was nothing more than a dirt strip. We pulled down to our spot, turned the plane into the wind, and hit the gas. As soon as we lifted off, we lost a jug on the right side. I looked back at the engine, and the pilot and I glanced at each other. The bad engine was shaking the plane hard. We considered our options and made a decision.

As the copilot, I went back to the jumpers and told them the situation. "We've lost a cylinder and can't get to the scheduled altitude. Once we land, the plane won't be able to take off again." I left off the part about how we didn't want to worry about finding an aircraft mechanic in Tahlequah, Oklahoma. "We're going to make a circle back over the field. I don't know how high we'll get. We're hoping for at least fifteen hundred feet, but we may not make it that high. Anyone who wants out, that's your time. Otherwise, we're taking this plane back to Meacham Field in Fort Worth for repairs."

They had about ten minutes to process that information and decide. When I came back, I told them we'd reached 1,200 feet and it was time. I opened the doors, and all but one jumped. That man rode back with us to Fort Worth, where we made a safe landing. It turned out to be a happy ending, but it could've been bad.

Like all illegal activities, the Sportsman's Travel Club finally drew the attention of the FAA. Shut down and with three big DC-3s to sell, the owners grew desperate. Scraping up what money they had, they decided to have two new engines installed in one of the DC-3s at a cut-rate repair shop in Wiley Post, Oklahoma. They had a potential buyer in Florida and needed the plane flown there. One of the plane's owners—a retired lieutenant colonel in the Air Force—asked if I wanted to fly the plane with him to Florida. I agreed. Another pilot flew us up to Wiley Post and dropped us off.

We tested the engines on the ground and they sounded good. But on takeoff, we blew a jug in the right side (I was starting to feel jinxed). The pilot/owner increased the throttle, pushing the left engine to the redline, then over. This was extremely dangerous and he knew it. These engines were brand new. They needed to be broken in. The plane was still headed to Florida when he noticed I was concerned.

"We've got to keep going," he told me. "I've got to get this airplane down to Florida."

Taking my hand off the controls, I turned to face him. "You can do that, sir, as soon as you drop me off at Meacham Field."

He studied my face and turned back to flying the plane. I gave him thirty seconds to see if the plane would change directions. It didn't. I looked at a gauge and saw the left engine overheating. This was getting serious.

Now I raised my voice. "Either we land at Meacham or I'll take over this airplane. I'm bigger than you. Believe me, I can handle it."

I studied his body for any sign of a decision. Seeing none, I clenched my fists and readied for a scuffle in the sky.

Chapter Six

I was young and tough, but I'd seen enough fights to know that older men still had a few tricks up their sleeves. They might conk a young stud over the head with an unseen leather blackjack or don a pair of brass knuckles to break a jaw. I didn't want to see what this pilot could do. Nor did I want to wrestle the controls from him. But I wasn't going to die like this.

My body tensed as I shifted my legs to stand up. That's when he sighed and made the turn. I checked the compass and, sure enough, we were headed south to Fort Worth. Throughout the short trip, I kept one eye on the left engine and the other on the pilot. He still might try to make Florida.

He didn't. And, wouldn't you know it, we lost the left engine as soon as the plane touched down. I shuddered to think where I'd have been if this had happened over the Gulf of Mexico. That's how desperate he was to sell the plane.

A few weeks later, I learned the Wortham brothers had gone in with Paul Pennington and purchased a twin-engine turboprop Commander. They hangared the plane at Fort Worth Meacham Field. Even though the plane didn't require a copilot, they wanted one to save the insurance money. They offered me the job if I'd fly for free. I needed the hours for my logbook, so I said yes.

As luck would have it, a turboprop just didn't cut it for up-and-coming developers and contractors. They added a Jet Commander, which *did* require a copilot. They agreed to pay me $75 per day, which wasn't much for a pilot, but way more than the $0 per day I had been getting.

One weekend, the pilot and I flew a twin-engine Beechcraft down to Mexico so I could walk the length of the paved airstrip. Sure enough, it would take their new Jet Commander. That meant trips to Mexico in a jet were now on the menu.

With so many Mexican trips under their belts, the Worthams were pros by now. They quickly paid off the local officials. This allowed us to pack the plane with money, guns, and *Playboy* magazines.

On our second trip down there, a local military commandant wanted to inspect the plane. He found everything. Unfortunately, he wasn't paid off. The Worthams had their hands in the air along with me and the pilot, waiting to see if we were headed back to some shithole jail. As the commandant's men leveled their machine guns at us, I wondered how much training these men had. What if one trigger finger slipped?

After some fake outrage and posturing, the commandant let us go. Coincidentally, his arms were wrapped around a case of real American Coca-Cola and several *Playboy* magazines. Apparently, he liked the articles, which he had to keep for evidence's sake.

After the first few trips, the Worthams realized that they didn't need to waste time finding acceptable women in Mexico when there were perfectly good ones in Texas. They began loading up the plane with gorgeous young women. Each trip down there had the plane rocking. We closed the cockpit curtain, but occasionally, I removed my headset to hear some of the antics back in the cabin. Those memories still linger.

It was in early April that we had a four-day trip scheduled. Thursday morning, I arrived early to have the plane pulled out to the tarmac. Like usual, the Wortham brothers arrived and climbed on board while the pilot and I loaded their luggage, weapons, and gear. When we finished, I looked out over the tarmac for the girls, who were usually chauffeured in a limo. Instead, I saw a Mercedes heading toward the plane. It screeched to a halt, spitting out two angry women. Without acknowledging our presence, they hustled up the stairs and into the cabin.

"Where are they?" one of the women asked.

"Where are who?" Billy Wortham replied to his wife.

"What are you talking about?" Willy chimed in. "Why are you here?"

"Why haven't you taken off?" one of the women asked the pilot.

"Uh, we're going through the checklist. That's mandatory before we turn on the engines."

I rubbed my hands together, looking out the window and hoping not to see the limo. I knew it would be here any second. Usually, the driver was ten minutes early. But for some reason, he was ten minutes late.

The two women looked over the situation, shook their heads, and deplaned. I watched them climb into their Mercedes and take off as Billy and Willy high-fived each other. No sooner had the Mercedes disappeared than the limo came speeding and weaving down the tarmac. Like something out of the movies, the driver put the limo into a sideways slide and rocketed from the car, hustling the girls onto the plane.

"Why were you late?" Billy asked him.

"I'm so sorry. The time moved ahead on Sunday, but I never changed my watch. I thought I had plenty of time, but I was wrong. I ran every red light picking up these girls and getting them here. Please don't fire me. I'll never let it happen again."

Billy handed him a hundred. "It's okay. You saved our ass this time."

The driver looked confused, but took the money and left. I filled him in later.

We took off, and soon, the plane was rocking. These Wortham boys sure knew how to party.

After that trip, Willy Wortham came up to the cockpit to discuss the near disaster. "What can we do to avoid a repeat of that situation?" he asked us.

The pilot rubbed his jaw. "We can keep the plane in the hangar with the doors closed. When we see the limo with the girls coming, we can have the line boys open a door to let it in. Then we can load the women on the plane and let the limo take off."

"Sounds good so far. Where do we come in?"

"We'll load the girls an hour early, let the limo leave, and wait for you. When you come, we'll open the doors, let you in, load your luggage real quick, and have the tug pull us out to the tarmac. Then we'll take right off. If anyone is watching, they won't see a thing."

"You know," Willy said, grinning, "I like the way you think. Make it happen." He was going to leave, but stopped and turned around. "Just so you know, these girls are aspiring young actresses between career opportunities. Okay?"

"Absolutely!" we said in unison. Whatever he wanted to call them. We never used the word "whore"—not once.

The new scheme worked well. The girls were always on the plane in the hangar and no one was the wiser.

Not to be left out, Paul Pennington used the plane when the Worthams didn't have it in Mexico. One of the main pilots was a bald man named Igor Dumas. We called him Dumbass, but pronounced it correctly when he was around. Dumbass and I flew Mr. Pennington and his main mistress, Silvia Slender, out to Las Vegas a lot. When I first saw her, I was stunned. She was drop-dead gorgeous. She was also a TCU debutante, and I wondered how I'd never crossed her path. Then again, I didn't own a jet airplane.

After several trips with Dumbass, I realized he was a thoroughly worthless pilot. Somehow, by the grace of God, he got the job done.

On one trip, we were told to fly Miss Slender out to West Texas to audition for a movie. Before we took the jet out there, I told him, "Dumas, I don't think that runway's going to handle this airplane. It's hot. It's asphalt and, *as you know*"—I'd learned to add that phrase to give the pilot's ego cover—"the Jet Commander has real small tires. They have a tiny footprint."

"So?" he said, needing me to connect more dots.

"Well, *as you know*, the tires hold a lot of weight grabbing that pavement. It's like taking off and landing on a sandy beach. The asphalt's going to give way because it's very pliable when it's hot. If we get stuck, they'll be taking that plane out in parts."

"We'll be fine," he said nonchalantly.

We landed in the scorching heat with thin plumes rising from the airstrip. My job was to get Miss Slender off the plane fast, which I did. As soon as she ducked into the waiting limo, I ran back to the luggage compartment, which was right under the jet engine, and fetched her bags. With those loaded, I started walking back to the plane and saw a sickening sight. Yelling, screaming, and doing back-flips, I could not get Dumbass's attention to move the plane. I ran up the stairs and ripped the headset off him. "Move the plane now!" I yelled. "We're sinking!"

He knew what I meant, but it was too late. To get the plane moving, I took over the controls and had to rock it back and forth before we hit the underlying dirt. Fortunately, the power of the jet freed us up. I got rolling right into a takeoff, leaving deep ruts behind. We heard later Mr. Pennington had to write a company check for $330,000 to fix that airstrip. And the worst part was that Miss Slender didn't get the part and had to fly back commercial—first class, of course.

Going back to the Worthams, they owned a ski-in-ski-out chalet in Aspen. As any pilot knows, Aspen is a nightmare. It's like flying into a box canyon. You can only take off one way, which is coming *out* of the canyon. But you must land going *into* the canyon. And if you ever lose an engine before touchdown and have to go around, planes like ours would never clear the mountains. It's a high-risk airport.

I quickly learned that to safely land in Aspen, we had to approach a different airport—Gunnison—then miss that approach, cancel our IFR flight plan with the Gunnison tower, and proceed up the canyon. I had to constantly remind myself to stay on the right side of the railroad track and road going up the canyon, because somebody was going to be coming out—which meant they'd be going the other way. That was Aspen.

I considered myself a top rate pilot. But one time, I failed to supervise Dumbass installing the drag chute. I knew the chute was important when we flew into Aspen since the high altitude limited our plane's stopping ability. Without a reliable backup hydraulics system, we always had to deploy the chute.

On this one trip, we landed with Mr. Pennington and Miss Slender in the back. As usual, Dumbass deployed the chute, but nothing happened. The plane was still hurtling down the runway, its speed unchecked.

I looked at Dumbass's eyes and they were big as saucers. He realized he'd forgotten to hook the chute up to the plane. His neatly packed bundle was drifting across the runway to the nearby forest, where it fluttered for a minute before settling into some pine trees. Without being able to take off safely, we slammed on the brakes and stopped two feet before the end of the runway. I know, because I measured it.

The tower called and shut down the airport. They sent out an airport truck to pick me up. As copilot, it was my job to go out and get the damned chute. It was snowing, so I had to bring it back to the hangar, where we hung it up from the rafters and waited for it to dry. Even so, I consider myself lucky to be able to tell that story.

That's the kind of crap a copilot has to put up with when he's trying to pick up hours for his logbook. Like all good stories, though, there's a happy ending.

Every time the plane had to be fueled, Dumbass paid for it using Wortham's company credit card. Some stations gave him S&H Green Stamps. Back then, these stamps could be collected and turned in for a wide variety of goods. Instead of handing them over to the Worthams, Dumbass went out and ordered home furnishings and other goodies. In fact, he planned the fuel stops at places that gave out S&H Green Stamps. He furnished his entire house with those stamps. Then it all came crashing down.

When I couldn't make a particular trip, another copilot sat in. That guy was less tolerant than I was, because he turned Dumbass in. Next thing I knew, the Worthams unexpectedly showed up at the hangar. Willy handled the dirty business. "I understand you've been getting a lot of S&H Green Stamps with the fuel purchases. What'd you do with them?"

Dumbass stammered, thinking of a good answer. "W-well, I put them into hangar improvements."

"Let's go see them," Willy said, clapping his hands together.

Of course, there weren't any hangar improvements. They fired him on the spot. That's how stupid he was. I would've said, "Gee, guys, I bought TVs and furniture for all of your mistresses. Since you want it, I'll go get your wives and show them where to pick it up. They'll love redecorating your mansion."

Dumbass didn't say that, so he was gone, and I got a new pilot to fly with—the copilot who had ratted him out.

How convenient.

Soon afterward, the new pilot and I loaded up the Worthams and their gaggle of girls, taking off for Vegas. They had learned from Mr. Pennington how much fun Vegas was.

We landed at McCarran and taxied to the hangar, where a limo waited. As soon as we opened the doors and sent the Worthams arm-in-arm with their hotties down the stairs, the limo doors flung open and out popped photographers, lawyers, and the two Mrs. Worthams. They had figured out we had to file flight plans with the FAA. This had led them to discover that their husbands weren't going to Mexico to hunt. The good news for the Worthams was that they were soon free to fly anywhere with all the girls they wanted. Unfortunately, they were a little light in the wallet, so they had to dump the planes—especially when Mr. Pennington's wife filed for divorce. At least I got some great stories out of it.

I went looking for a job and hunted down my old bosses at the air travel club. I learned they had been shot down in Mexico trying to leave with a load of drugs. The plane had crashed and they'd died. So I sat down at my desk and scratched their names off my list of possible employers.

Even though I was flying a lot professionally, Big T still had his hooks in me. Twice a year, I had to fly to his 335-acre ranch in Rio Vista, located an hour south of Fort Worth. Dad was a gentleman farmer—with a hundred head of cattle, some pigs, goats, and chickens, one horse, and one illegal Mexican, Austeen, whom I'd picked up in Mexia. Dad used some of the acres to raise hay, which he fed to his animals. Usually, there was too much hay. He sold the surplus to the locals for extra spending money.

The ranch was situated well off the road, with three streams and three natural holding tanks. A third of it was heavily forested. This allowed Austeen to grow some marijuana and keep it hidden from prying eyes. Austeen used the income from those sales to send money back to his family in Mexico.

Twice a year, when Dad told me it was time, I flew the Aero Commander 200 feet over the nearby towns of Blum and Covington, signaling the local boys that work was available at Big T's ranch. Then I'd touch down in Rio Vista at a fly-in bank. They had a nice airstrip for clients to land and make deposits. After I secured the plane, someone from the ranch would come and pick me up. Then it was work time—*hard* work time.

If the hay had been cut, I worked with the local boys, baling and loading it into a large barn the size of an airplane hangar. Meanwhile, Austeen would be on the horse rounding up the cattle for deworming and shots—all the stuff a gentleman farmer has to be concerned with.

One time, Dad was working in a chute behind a cow, shoving a large pill the size of a fist up its backside. He must have hit a nerve, because the cow jolted forward, busting down the stall I sat in and tossing me back ten feet. It was quite a knock. I remember lying there wishing I was a professional pilot so I didn't have to do this crap.

Usually, Dad drove down. But when he flew, the bank president would give him a ride to the ranch. The townspeople knew Big T because Mom's family was from nearby Covington. Her sister's husband ran the waterworks there, and her other sister had left Oakland with her husband to live in Covington because their daughter was brutally murdered. They'd fled California to rural Texas, where locals wore pistols on their hips and had long guns mounted on their pickup's rear window. They knew that Texans took care of their own problems.

I always got a kick flying over these small towns. Just off a dirt road, I'd see two men in rocking chairs outside the barbershop smoking cigars. They were just telling stories and killing time.

As for my time at Rio Vista, the hard work kept the weight off. Baling hay even honed my taut physique. That was the only good thing about it.

Over time, Dad's lighting business boomed and he didn't get down to the ranch much. One day, the cows came down with Bangs disease, an infectious bacterium that causes spontaneous abortions. The dog started eating the chickens. The pigs were eating their young. The place got too big for Austeen, who had other distractions like rolling joints. It was time to sell.

Dad found a young couple who wanted to live there and work the farm. Shortly after they closed on the loan and Big T got his money, the farmhouse burned down. I didn't ask too many questions after that.

Big T's base of operations was the fourplex in Euless he owned, and the Western Hills Inn. Marilyn Crenshaw kept all that running. However, Dad wanted to have a southern base of operations, closer to Mexico. That's why he bought a swank fourplex in Rancho Viejo—an upscale, gated development. Located halfway between Harlingen and Brownsville in the Rio Grande Valley, Rancho Viejo had a swim-up bar, clubhouse, and two world-class golf courses. One of the courses—Diablo—held PGA qualifying events.

Big T used Rancho Viejo to give mayors, clients, and businessmen a place to let their hair down. It was close to the beach and South Padre Island. Guests could go deep sea fishing. The hunting was good too. They could also drive to Mexico and visit Boy's Town in Matamoros. Anything they wanted to do, Rancho Viejo and Big T could provide it.

Dad liked the spot because nearby Harlingen was home to the Confederate Air Force. After becoming friends with war heroes such as Pappy Boyington of the Black Sheep Squadron, we could fly vintage World War Two aircraft. It was a great time, although it's now called the *Consolidated* Air Force.

Dad kept a car permanently parked at the airport, which was very convenient. I'd fly guests down there and drop them off. Sometimes I stayed there too. When no one was using the fourplex, Big T rented it out to bring in more cash for his operation. It was true that he had his fingers in a lot of pies.

Between flying professionally and all the runs I made for Big T, the years raced by. One day, I woke up and discovered I'd graduated cum laude from the University of Texas at Arlington with a bachelor's degree in business administration. I'd been on the Dean's List the entire time at UTA, never studying for a test. School had been easy. Now it was over. I needed a job, but I also needed to figure out how to become a pilot for one of the national airlines. It was time to put my college-educated brain to work.

Chapter Seven

Hanging out at the airports and talking to pilots, I learned there was a position open. The chief pilot for Shenandoah Oil, who I knew, said he needed a new copilot. The pay was $18,000 per year. I was twenty years old and couldn't say yes fast enough.

Interestingly, Big T had some connections with Shenandoah Oil. First, the company was based in downtown Fort Worth. One of the principal investors, Jimmy Stewart, the famous actor, owned a lot of property around Possum Kingdom Lake, some of it gas-producing. Big T just happened to have a lake cabin there. When Dad built it, he poured a slab, unlike almost every other house on the lake that sat on posts. As plumbing came to the lake, he didn't want to bust open the slab. The best way to avoid doing that was to elevate the toilet to fit a p-trap underneath. Steps were then built to make it easy to get up to the toilet. Basically, he created a toilet throne. Each time I used it, I felt like a king. And because I was Big T's son, I was a *prince*. But I digress.

Near Dad's cabin, there happened to be an airstrip. It was owned by the Jimmy Stewart family. Big T had to get Mr. Stewart's permission to land his plane there. Then he had to rent a couple of Bobcats and knock out a taxiway from the runway to the back end of the cabin. (That runway is still there at the northwest end of Possum Kingdom Lake.) With the taxiway built, I'd fly the Twin Aero Commander in there when Big T needed something dropped off or picked up. The Toler family were the only ones besides Jimmy Stewart who used the runway. Because of this, we maintained the airstrip *and* good relations with Jimmy Stewart.

In working for Shenandoah Oil, I flew a different class of mission. They did a lot of exploratory stuff along the Gulf Coast, but their big find was in Guatemala. It was a very sizeable oil field. We flew their Learjet to Guatemala City quite often, and the journey wasn't always without incident.

One trip happened two days after they had experienced a 7.3 earthquake. Thirty thousand lives were lost. When we arrived, they were still having aftershocks reaching 6.5. That was my first experience with earthquakes.

The purpose of that trip was to inspect the oil field for damage. Since they had no way to get the oil out, they intended to raise money to build a pipeline from their oil find to the seaport. This trip would let them see how the terrain looked and if that was still feasible.

Landing in Guatemala City, we dodged large potholes and fissures on the runway. The locals had told us the runway was clear before we'd taken off from Fort Worth, but it was worse than we expected. Still, we did land safely and all of us got to the hotel. "Us" consisted of Shenandoah's president, an engineer, one of the president's executives, the pilot, and me.

Driving through downtown, we saw many of the buildings were flattened due to the unreinforced masonry used to build them. Most of the loss of life had occurred when the buildings fell, crushing the families inside. It was a horrible way to go.

We stayed in the only hotel open. After they took our money, the clerk explained that management had closed the lower five floors because they were heavily damaged and unsafe. They claimed the floors above the fifth floor were safe because the flex point was there—whatever that meant. They put us on the seventh floor—two floors above the damage.

That first night, a 5.6 aftershock hit. I ran down the stairs with one leg in a pair of pants and the other leg hanging out. I just wanted to get outside alive.

All five of us made it to the ground floor, along with a couple on their honeymoon. They had a large bottle of scotch in their hands, which they happily shared. We sat by the pool, sipping scotch and watching our worries dissolve away.

A local hanging out by the pool told me she had been staying in a room on our floor. I asked her if she was going back upstairs. "No!" she said adamantly.

"Then that means I'm not going either," I announced. I'd traveled enough to know that if the locals weren't doing something, I shouldn't be doing it either.

We slept on the lounge chairs, awakening to the sounds of Guatemalans rebuilding their city. It was quite sobering.

The three company employees scrounged up a car and left the hotel, spending the day assessing the damage and what it would take to get the pipeline built. When they returned, the pilot and I decided to spend the night in the airplane. No way were we staying in that hotel again.

When it was time to fly out, we talked to the tower about the runway's condition. They sent out a truck to inspect it. The second they cleared us, we headed down the runway, which ended at the edge of a cliff. Dodging potholes and large fissures, we barely got airborne before running out of pavement. As soon as I knew we were going to make it, a shiver ran down my spine. It had been a rough trip, one I was grateful to make it home safely.

The great aspect about working for Shenandoah Oil was five o'clock on Friday. If we made it to that point without a mission, we were guaranteed the weekend off. During the week, though, we were always on call.

We flew missions all over the U.S. We also made several trips to Milwaukee, Wisconsin—the headquarters of the Associated Milk Producers. Jimmy Stewart was a director and had to attend board meetings.

The first time I saw Mr. Stewart was March 3, 1976. I remember it well, because he came up to me and said, "Oh, I'm Jimmy Stewart."

I was starstruck, having grown up seeing his movies. For twenty-five cents, I'd seen the 1965 movie *Shenandoah*. It was a great film. (In fact, he took the profits from that movie and funded the oil company.) Now, it was the 1970s, and Mr. Stewart was all over the television. He was a pleasure to pilot around.

At eight o'clock one evening, I received an emergency call. I was told that Jimmy Stewart's best friend and chief financial advisor was extremely sick. I raced to the plane and fueled it up. When the pilot arrived, I had the plane pulled out and ready to go.

We blasted out of there and began a climb to 41,000 feet. The air is thin up there. We'd burn less fuel. We'd also be above the jet stream, avoiding any headwinds. Just as we reached our designated altitude, we had an explosive decompression. I glanced at the panel. The cabin was at a pressure of 34,000 feet—an altitude that provides nine seconds of consciousness for anyone not breathing oxygen through a mask.

I figured we'd lost a flow-control valve, which cut off pressurized air into the cabin. It was like the Payne Stewart incident, where everyone on board died due to lack of oxygen. Just in case this happened, we wore quick-donning masks loosely around our necks. As the alarm sounded, we pulled the masks away from our heads, releasing two elastic straps that jerked them back tight to our face. This automatically opened the flow of fresh oxygen. Both of us had trained for such an event, but this was the first time it had happened to me on a flight.

We immediately descended and made an emergency landing at Midland. It was there that we made a sobering discovery: that Learjet model didn't have quick-donning masks for passengers. If Jimmy Stewart and his friend had been on board, they would've likely died.

Midland was a great place to land. Several large oil companies were based there. That meant they had their Learjets parked at the airport, with plenty of extra flow-control valves in stock. A mechanic came out that night and installed it for us. After adding more oxygen and testing it out, we tore out of there and made it to Los Angeles just in time for our morning pickup.

I was freshening up the cabin when a limo dropped off Jimmy Stewart and his friend at the plane. I could see his friend was in bad shape. Jimmy was distraught because of this. We got them situated in the back and took off.

Just outside of Los Angeles, I turned to the pilot with an idea. "I know Jimmy Stewart used to be in the Army Air Corps. Why don't we let him sit up here while I sit back there with his buddy? It might help take his mind off the situation."

The pilot agreed. I went back and told Mr. Stewart (we called the passengers by their formal names) about my idea. It was a great move. He loved sitting up there.

As for me, talking to his friend was like talking to someone with Alzheimer's. No matter how many times I told him my name was Tom, he asked me a dozen more times, "What's your name again?" Or he'd tell me the same story over and over and over. I could only imagine what Jimmy had been going through. It must have been gut-wrenching.

Just outside of Denver, I had to tap Mr. Stewart on the shoulder so we could land in Denver to add fuel. He went back to his friend and I took my copilot seat. After landing, the pilot decided to stay with the airplane. He asked me to take Mr. Stewart to the pilots' lounge there at Combs Gates and shield him from the gawkers and lookers. I gladly did that, sitting with him in the pilots' lounge until the airplane was refueled. Thankfully, everyone left him alone. When the pilot gave me the signal, we got back on the airplane and took off.

The trip was relatively smooth. As we approached the airport in Rochester, Minnesota, we received a weather report: a temperature of nine degrees with a forecast high of thirteen. It had been like that for a week. Mr. Stewart had thought ahead, because he and his friend were bundled up in thick overcoats. I hadn't. After all, when we left Fort Worth, the temperature was in the seventies. Even Los Angeles was in the seventies. I hadn't realized that the Mayo Clinic was in Minnesota. That's why I exited the aircraft in my open-collared golf shirt, pulling a thin leather jacket tight around my tan frame. *Welcome to Minnesota.*

I stood on the tarmac, watching the limo whisk Mr. Stewart and his friend away. On the edges of the airfield, I spotted patches of snow permanently frozen into the landscape. All I could think of was how quickly I could get to the pilots' lounge without slipping and breaking something.

As copilot, my job was to get the plane refueled and the interior cleaned up. It had to look nice. Although there was a portable toilet on board, it was rarely used since we had to stop so often for fuel. At least I had that good news to celebrate.

I went back inside the plane and cleaned it up. The residual heat comforted me, but with the door open and the engines off, the cabin turned into a meat freezer. That's why I hustled back down the stairs and toward the pilots' lounge.

Once inside, I learned there was no pilots' lounge. Instead, I found the pilot hanging out at the flight office, which occupied one end of the hangar. As I stood there trying to get warm, I saw the fuel truck roll up to the plane. I knew it was my job to watch him fill it up, as fuel truck operators were known to occasionally fudge the numbers. When you were in the air and realized you'd been duped, what were you going to do? Turn around? I doubt it. And God forbid if you ran out of fuel. So, I should've been watching every drop hit the tank, but it was too damn cold. I just couldn't do it. Instead, I hung out in the flight office, waiting for the fuel vendor to bring in the receipt, where I would check the gallons pumped and see if that matched up with what I expected.

When he arrived, I checked it over and everything seemed fine. The clerk calculated the price and took a company credit card from the pilot. It was then that I decided to brave the cold and go out to inspect the four fuel caps. I needed to make sure they had been put on correctly.

As I neared the plane, I noticed it listing to one side. Suddenly, red hydraulic fluid squirted out of the landing struts. I watched, helpless, as the plane lowered to the tarmac, stopping a few inches before it hit the pavement. Then it dawned on me: We'd been flying to mostly southern destinations, including Central America. The seals were conditioned to warmer temperatures, and they were older. Sure, the seals experienced super-cold temps at 41,000 feet, but they weren't supporting a load when they were tucked in the wheel wells. When we landed in Minnesota, our tanks were almost empty. There was less weight. The seals were supporting a very light load. Only with the combination of cold temperatures *and* heavy fuel tanks did the seals fail.

Seeing this disaster, I ran back into the office to tell the pilot. We shook our heads and considered the options.

Our plan was for Mr. Stewart to escort his friend to the hospital and get him checked in. When that was done, he'd return to the plane and we'd fly him home to Los Angeles. With the plane inches above the pavement, that plan didn't look so good.

Back then, there was no air service in Rochester. The only equipment they had to move an airplane was an old-timey farm tractor with the little tires up front and the great big ones in the back. All it could do was pull the plane forward very slowly.

The pilot and I decided there was nothing we could do on the tarmac. We had a line boy hook up the tractor to the plane and try to pull it into the hangar. Once it was there, we could sort out a plan of action.

The tarmac was fairly flat. The plane moved well. But an imposing icy ramp leading to the hangar stopped us cold. The tractor couldn't get the job done.

I ran out there and started pushing on the right wing. The pilot followed, taking the left wing. Out of nowhere, Jimmy Stewart put his hands on my wing and another line boy helped the pilot. With two men on each wing and the tractor barely pulling the plane, somehow we made it.

"Can we take off?" Mr. Stewart asked when the plane came to a stop.

"No, sir," the pilot replied. "The landing struts will punch a hole through the wings. Somehow, we'll have to inflate the struts."

But how?

The plane was fueled up. There was no safe and easy way to take the fuel out and lighten the load. Even if we did, we couldn't take off without fuel.

We looked around the hangar and spotted a massive flame-throwing burner. We grabbed some other portable heaters, lighting them on high. After we closed the large doors, the hangar warmed up nicely.

When the temperature reached the upper seventies for thirty minutes, the gaskets expanded. Now that they could temporarily hold a seal, we looked around for something to put in there.

Hydraulic fluid was out of the question, since they didn't have any and we didn't have the ability to get it into the struts. We spotted a nitrogen bottle. That might work.

We asked the line boys if they had a reduction valve to minimize the gas coming from a 2000 psi bottle. If we put that up to the strut and cranked it open, we'd permanently blow out the seal. Then we'd need to fly in a mechanic, which would take days. Unfortunately, the line boys didn't have a reduction valve. Our only option was to milk the bottle and allow a tiny bit in during each burst. All we needed was 10 psi in each strut. This would take a steady hand.

The only other issue we had to avoid was getting blown up. That would mean Jimmy Stewart would get to permanently experience *It's a Wonderful Life*. The pilot and I looked at each other and nodded.

"Mr. Stewart," the pilot said, "this is going to be dangerous. You have a career. Please go and hang out in the flight office. We'll come get you if it works."

And if it doesn't—well, you can contact our next of kin.

It worked. We loaded him up and taxied him out of the hangar, praying each seal would hold long enough to get airborne. Since we had already gained clearance for takeoff, we punched it hard and lifted off without a problem. When we lowered the struts for a landing at Los Angeles, we prayed they worked again.

They did. We made it back to Fort Worth Meacham Field, where the plane underwent an overhaul of the struts. It was a close call.

Mr. Stewart told us he was amazed by our ingenuity. He thanked us profusely. I found him to be a very gracious man.

The next week, we repeated the trip, taking Mr. Stewart up to Minnesota to collect his friend. When we landed in Los Angeles, Mr. Stewart came and shook my hand, thanking me for being a friend. He was so appreciative of me giving up my seat so that he could sit up front and fly the airplane that he brought out a special picture of himself and autographed it to me. We talked for a little bit, and he told me he was a retired brigadier general. I couldn't believe it. I really enjoyed his company.

Unfortunately, the Mayo Clinic couldn't help his friend. He died shortly after that. It was a tough thing for Mr. Stewart to take. And it was hard for me to see up close. I wished it could've turned out better.

Unlike the Wortham brothers, Shenandoah Oil was a first-class company. They had all sorts of great shareholders like Julie Andrews and Jimmy Stewart. There were no shenanigans, no aspiring actresses between career opportunities, no guns, and no private detectives. I was happy to be flying professionally and making a living in the air, although it was meager.

At the same time, I applied to the large carriers for a better-paying job. Each day, I checked the mail for a letter, but none came. I'd have to keep trying and hoping.

Now that I had hauled Mr. Stewart on at least ten missions, I felt I knew him well. Landing at his airstrip in Possum Kingdom Lake with one of Big T's planes seemed like coming home to family—at least in my mind. Dad, though, looked at it as nothing more than business. He took more trips out there than I did, since he had important men to take fishing and gambling.

On one trip, he took his secretary, Marilyn Crenshaw, out there in his Cessna 172. The story was that they were taking supplies to the cabin. It had to be well stocked for the VIPs he brought out there. I'm not sure if he spent the night or a few hours with Marilyn at the cabin. Whatever it was, they had finished and were back on the plane ready to come home. Dad cranked on the engine and had the blades spinning when Marilyn realized she'd forgotten something in the cabin. She climbed out and went to fetch it. As she proceeded back to the plane, she wasn't paying attention and walked right into the prop. Her ear-piercing scream rocked my dad to his core. This single event would change Big T's empire and life as we knew it.

Chapter Eight

The boat rolled side to side as the beam sea continued its mostly southern direction. Breakers no longer crashed onto the fly bridge. Until an hour ago, I'd been heading into the waves to avoid being toppled. But the seas had calmed just enough so I could head more easterly and make better time until I saw land.

The windscreen was caked with salt. If my helper below ever woke up, I'd need him to draw some fresh water from the 130-gallon tank and heat it up. Once it was good and hot, he'd have to toss it over the windscreen to break down the salt. But he wasn't up and I couldn't yell for him. I'd have to make do.

I studied the instrument panel. The compass was still unreadable, forcing me to continue navigating by the stars, which were out in full. At least I could see though a small opening at the top of the windscreen. It wasn't covered over. That was something to be thankful for.

I glanced down and saw Duke. He was intently focused on keeping me awake. Like me, he hadn't moved. A small divot at the tip of my left Croc had grown, evidence that he'd been doing his job.

I looked over at the first mate's chair next to me and jumped. "Beverley! What are you doing here?"

"I heard you were having some trouble and needed help. After all, I was your copilot at one time. Remember?"

I blinked several times, hardly believing the tall, thin blonde was on my boat. "Yeah, I remember those days. I also seem to remember you were my girlfriend too."

She pushed back her long hair. "Well, that's true. But you did pretty good for yourself. I seem to remember you meeting another blonde a few years later." She grinned. "So, what's the problem here?"

I tapped the instrument panel. "My starboard engine isn't working. Either the shaft or propeller is damaged, or something inside the engine has let loose. My port engine is all I have. If I lose that, I'll drift down to Cuba or more likely capsize. I've tried using the emergency alert system, but no one's responding to my calls. My only option is to stay awake so I can keep the boat pointed toward land and avoid any large waves. I figure I have at least seven more hours to go. Of course, I'd love it if you could fix that engine."

"I can't do that. But I can keep you awake, maybe give Duke here a break. Why don't you tell me what happened to that poor girl—Marilyn Crenshaw, I think you called her? That story caught my attention."

"Oh yeah. Well, Marilyn walked into the prop. With one clip, the blade severed her left arm just below the elbow. Because it was at idle speed, the cut wasn't clean—it pulled some of the flesh and muscle out. With her limb lying on the ground a few feet away, she stopped in her tracks, probably in shock. Dad cut the engine and jumped out, wrapping his belt tight around the stub. He picked up the severed arm, putting it on ice. Then he jumped in the pickup and drove her to a decent hospital in Graham. They couldn't save her arm but did save her life. It was tragic."

"You said this changed Big T. I never noticed anything."

"Marilyn ran his world. He trusted her completely. After the accident, it was the beginning of a long slide down. He started losing his golden touch along with his business. I can't say behind every great man is a good woman, because really, he was the front man for a sharp operator in the background. At least, that's the way I saw it."

"Wow! That's tough, Tom. But if I recall, right around that same time, our flight careers almost ended before they could even get started. Remember?"

"Yes," I chuckled. "I sure do. Why don't you talk for a while? I could use a break. Maybe tell Duke how you ended up in Fort Worth and how we started dating. Then you can get into our careers."

"I can do that. Let's see, where do I start? …"

… As a little girl, I was obsessed with flying. When my mother pushed me around in a stroller, I'd reach up at the planes flying overhead, trying to snatch them from the sky. I was sure I could catch them. When that didn't work, I grew up a little and tried to fly myself.

One balmy afternoon in Fort Myers, my parents took me to this home across the street. There, they plopped me down on a couch. They enjoyed having drinks with this old couple. In Florida, afternoon cocktails were routine.

That first time, I spotted this statue of a man with wings. The old couple told me it was Icarus. Icarus had been a prisoner in a tower when his father built him a set of wings made of feathers and wax. This allowed Icarus to jump from the tower and fly to freedom. That seemed like a wonderful idea to me.

The next time I visited, they let me hold the statue. I sat there studying his wax wings, falling in love with the idea of flying. I can't explain it; at four years old, I simply wanted to be airborne.

After that second visit, we went home. When my parents had settled into their usual spots in the living room, I took the opportunity to slip into the kitchen. There, I found my own tower—a washing machine. Standing on top, I spread my wings and jumped off, willing myself to fly across the floor. It was less of a flight and more of a dive. I did it several more times, always ending up in a heap. But I was tough and determined. I survived.

When I wasn't jumping off the washing machine, I loved watching planes land. I always tried to talk someone—usually Aunt Ginger—in to taking me to a chain-link fence by the airport so I could watch planes land at night. She seemed to get a kick out of watching me enjoy the view.

One weekend, my parents traveled to Miami, leaving me in Aunt Ginger's care. As we drove north on Fort Myers' main drag, I spotted a sign on the side of the road: *Airplane Flights: A Penny a Pound.* I weighed seventy-five pounds, so I knew I needed three quarters. My aunt wouldn't let me go because she was responsible for me. Back in those days, I couldn't pick up a cell phone to call my parents because it hadn't been invented yet. I was sunk. That was the only fight I ever had with Aunt Ginger. Boy, was I mad.

When I turned sixteen, I begged my father to let me take a flying lesson. He refused. I was an only child, tasked with helping out in a family side business. He didn't want me distracted.

We owned and operated a ranch where we raised, trained, and showed registered quarter horses. Our ranch was six miles from the house. As a working owner, Dad woke up each morning and drove to the ranch. He cleaned the stalls and fed the horses before heading in to his day job. After school, I would go there to clean out the stalls and ride and exercise the horses. We had a kitchen area set up there. While Dad and I worked the horses, Mom came over and cooked dinner. Then we'd all sit down and eat. It was terrific fun. I loved all of it.

Before we bought the ranch and the horses, Dad sat me down and explained the rules. "If I ever see that you're losing interest in the horses *or* you've finished high school and decide to go off to college away from here, the ranch will be sold. Do you understand?"

"Yes, Dad," I promised. "I won't lose interest."

He was smart. As a male, he knew what could happen to a young girl. He also knew that taking care of horses was all-consuming. I wouldn't have time for boys or drugs or flying lessons.

It worked out just like he planned. My parents would pick me up Friday afternoon from school, our Bonneville packed and pulling a fully loaded horse trailer. We'd take off for a horse show in another town. While my friends were going to dances and parties, we were far away competing for prizes. No guys. No drugs. No problems.

I went through most of high school like this until one fateful day. Instead of taking care of the horses, I decided to go to a local hangout with my friends. I already knew my dad wasn't going out to the ranch that afternoon. There was no way he'd catch me. When I came home from the hangout, he asked me, "How are the horses?"

"Oh, you know," I said, refusing to make eye contact, "they're great." I assumed he wouldn't know I'd just lied to him.

The next morning, he went out there and saw the stalls were extra dirty and the horses antsy. Checking the rakes and hay and tools, he saw everything was just how he'd left it the previous morning. He knew I'd never been there.

That day, he went to work and put the ranch on the market. When my mother and I found out, we sat in the living room sobbing, begging him to change his mind. He silently shook his head. Two weeks later, the precious horses were gone along with the ranch. He'd meant what he said. That was one tough man.

Raising and showing horses is expensive. Yet we didn't have money growing up. During my elementary years, Dad owned the Flamingo Package Store—a tiny liquor shop the size of a bedroom. I was in the third grade when the teacher asked us to write down our father's profession. (Back then, mothers didn't work.) I was too embarrassed to put down liquor store owner. When Dad found out, he immediately went to real estate school and changed professions.

From the first moment of his new career, things were bad. He didn't make one dime his first year. We'd already planned a family trip to Colorado, yet we were dead broke. I was so excited and, as I was an only child, he didn't want to disappoint me. We shouldn't have gone, but we did. I had a blast, never knowing the precarious financial position we were in as we spent our last bit of money. Incredibly, he closed on his first deal when we returned home—a really big one. From that day forward, he did well. So well that he negotiated a great deal for the horse ranch we later sold.

Like Tom's father, my dad was a Navy man. But the comparisons stop there. He joined the service at seventeen and worked in the Brooklyn Navy Yards, unable to attend college when he got out. The main reason was money. The second reason was a woman.

Mom was a native New Yorker while Dad was a third-generation Fort Myers. Worlds collided when he brought her down to Fort Myers. The second she stepped off the train dressed New York style—long coat and a hat with a feather—my dad's parents stared at her like she was an alien from Mars. My grandmother cried out loud, saying, "Bob, what have you done? Have you lost your mind? This is a New York showgirl!"

To Mom's credit, she was tough. She forced herself to adapt to his lifestyle. One example was a hunting camp they leased in the Everglades for over sixty years. Dad would cut down a palm tree and chop up the leaves so Mom could make swamp cabbage. She was so in love with him that she learned to cook grits and anything else he wanted. He loved to fish, so she went with him. They did everything together. Eventually, my grandparents grew to adore her, as Mom had become a true Southerner.

With a great woman behind him, my working-class father climbed the ladder of success, one calloused hand after another. When I graduated from Fort Myers High School, Dad could afford to send me to Europe to study and pick up some college credits. I toured cities and countries, drinking in the antiquity of Europe. Plus, I loved flying over there. When I returned, it was time to attend college. But which one?

All the kids from my graduating class went to SEC schools like Florida, Alabama, Georgia, and Auburn. Yet I had my eye trained westward, to Texas. How had that happened?

Each year, we drove to Estes Park in Colorado for our family vacation. Along the way, we always stopped in the Dallas/Fort Worth area. The first time is embedded in my memory. We had dinner at a steak place and they served something on the side called Texas toast. When the meal arrived, there on a plate was this inch-thick slab of white toast. Its sides had been brushed with butter and grilled to a light-brown perfection. Like Icarus's wings, Texas was a place that fascinated me.

Whenever we drove to Colorado, I dreamed of Texas toast. And all the horses and cows there were a bonus, especially with my experience in the business. Dad also played golf with a man who had graduated from a college in Texas. The man's wife had gone to the same college, and they filled me with all sorts of good thoughts. By the time I graduated, I decided that their college sounded fun, so I told my parents I was going to TCU. Now I was Fort Worth–bound thanks to Dad's golfing buddy and Texas toast.

My parents and I flew into Love Field. As we walked into the rental car place, it started hitting me. Before, I'd been so excited to come here even though I'd never seen the campus. Now, reality was setting in. Mom and Dad were going to get me settled into college and then leave me behind. I didn't know anybody. My mind filled with fear.

The rental car clerk said, "What are you out here for?" My father told him I was attending TCU. "Oh, that's great," the clerk said. "I hope you like Mexican food."

With the weight of this situation fully upon my shoulders, I snapped back at him. "I've never heard of Mexican food and I'm pretty sure I won't like it." This was 1970. In Florida, the only thing close was Cuban food. I was in for a Texas education.

At TCU, we did our best to find our way around. We bought the necessities: an electric typewriter, school supplies, and toiletries. Everything a college student would need. Someone had told my parents back home that when we got to Fort Worth, we had to eat at a place called Joe T. Garcia's for lunch. So off we went in search of the mystical restaurant.

We drove through Cowtown, looking and looking, navigating some rickety roads made with bricks. Finally, we spotted a building listing to one side, about to fall down. Outside, a line of people wrapped around the block.

"I'm not eating there," I said. "I'm not eating in a building that's falling down."

Dad was very impatient and hated waiting for anything. We left and found another place to eat. Joe T. Garcia's would have to wait.

By now, all the kids had checked into the dorm except me. I was the last one. That evening, Mom and Dad stood by the rental car in the parking lot, waiting to say goodbye. Mom put her sunglasses on, but I could still see the tears running down her face.

Feeling the enormity of all this, I blurted out, "How can you leave me at this prison when you have each other? I don't have anybody!"

Dad calmly reached into his coat pocket and produced an envelope, handing it to me. They hugged me and drove off, leaving me completely alone.

I staggered to my room and opened the envelope. It was a one-way ticket home on Braniff. Once again, it was the smartest thing he could've done. He knew how obstinate I was. No matter what, I wasn't going to use that ticket. But if he'd said to me, "You can't come home until Christmas. You've got to stay here at least until Christmas," I would've been home the next week. They used reverse psychology.

I didn't use that ticket until the first semester ended, because it was understood that I would go home for Christmas. When I waddled off the airplane, my mother wasn't sure it was me. I'd gained eighteen pounds from eating Mexican food at Joe T. Garcia's! She was freaking out at my round face. For some reason, those nice Texas girls had taught me how to eat Mexican food. They'd taken a skinny Florida girl and fattened her up. By the end of my college career, every time my parents came to visit, they had to hit Joe T. Garcia's. Only then did they fully understand the lure of Mexican food.

With my freshman year over and the horses gone, I was determined to fly. And I'm not talking jumping off a washing machine. My father could see my desire and stopped fighting me. The odd thing about this obsession was that no one in my family had any connection whatsoever with flying or the aviation industry. They flew on commercial airlines like the rest of us. I guess Dad decided to have what control he could by funding my obsession. I was fine with that, so long as I could fly.

My first lesson was in Fort Myers with Eddie Wilson. He was the one who had set up that sign advertising flights at a penny a pound. Now I weighed more than seventy-five pounds and he most certainly charged more than seventy-five cents.

I took all the lessons I could cram into one summer. When I did my first solo, I rented an airplane and told Mom what time I'd be flying over the house. Sure enough, she was standing in the driveway waving at me as I flew circles overhead. By the time I was ready to go back to college, I was working on my private pilot's license.

My flight instructor happened to know about a flight school—Acme—in Fort Worth at Meacham Field. I went looking for it and found Aviation Corporation of Texas (Av-Tex) instead. I eventually worked there as a secretary to fund some of my flying. That's where I met the handsome Tom Toler and we started dating.

Early on, he handed me his resume and asked for some help. I saw the date of birth and told him, "We need to correct that. You're not the same age as me."

"No, that's right," he said.

I couldn't believe it. He had so much more experience in the plane than I did. With the way he acted, I was sure he was at least five years older—if not more. It was stunning. Our love of flying connected us.

From the outside, someone might have thought that I was using him. He had access to much better planes than I did. And he was always picking up better jobs. I would never use someone like that, but I did learn an incredible lot about flying when we were together.

However, it was one trip to Florida that almost ended our careers. We were flying from the Miami area to Page Field—where I took my flying lessons—when a nasty thunderstorm popped up. Rain slammed into the windshield and winds tossed us all around. I was in the copilot's seat when my door popped open. That's when I remembered Icarus. In college, I'd learned his wings melted when he flew too close to the sun, dropping him into the ocean where he drowned. They named that body of water the Icarian Sea. I wondered if Tom and I were headed for Icarus's fate.

Chapter Nine

The Comanche 250 bounced up and down violently. The situation was critical. With my door open, it was nearly impossible to communicate with Tom or the controller. I tried several times to close it but couldn't. The outside wind pressure was too fierce to open the door far enough to get a good pull. And the wind wasn't strong enough to close it for me. Landing the plane was our only option.

I looked over at Tom and he had his hands full. The wheel had a mind of its own. It took a tremendous effort to maintain control.

"We've got to land!" Tom screamed. I heard some of what he said and read his lips to fill in the blanks. "Is there any place we can put this thing down? Because we're going down!"

I had grown up in this area, especially at the hunting lease directly below us. "Start looking off your left wing!" I yelled back. "There's an old Air Force base there."

He craned his neck to look for the airstrip. When the plane tilted to his side, Tom could see it. He pushed the yoke forward and we descended rapidly on an emergency VFR approach. The crosswind let up just enough for the plane to hit the runway at the threshold. The second we touched down, I let out a huge sigh. That was close.

The old Air Force base had been converted to a municipal airport for the town of Immokalee. After parking the plane and shaking ourselves off, we walked across the street to grab some lunch. By the time we finished, the thunderstorm had passed over, leaving nothing but clear blue skies. We took off for my parents' home in Fort Myers, arriving safely but late.

During my last year at TCU, I looked for any job that put me in the air. Because he was so far ahead of me, Tom snagged the decent jobs while I got the leftovers. And even though the seventies were a coming out party for women, we still had a lot of catching up to do when it came to career opportunities. When a job came through Av-Tex and the guys didn't want it, they said, "Pass it down to Bev—she'll want it." I did.

My first paying job came as I sat in the office with the owner of an old 1953 Bonanza D35. We watched as a mortician drove up and came inside. He needed someone to fly a body to Hope, Arkansas. Tom and the rest of the men were off working charter flights. It was just me and the owner. I said, "I'll do it!"

At that point, I had a total of 300 hours. The problem was, I needed 500 hours to qualify for the owner's insurance. I was thrilled when he called his insurance company and got a waiver for me to fly that trip.

The mortician explained that the body was that of a nineteen-year-old girl who had died of an overdose. She had been embalmed. I glanced outside at the approaching dusk. It would be dark soon. I needed to get in the air and rip off some mileage.

The girl was six feet tall on a short stretcher. I had to load her through the cargo door, angling and twisting the stretcher to make her fit. This caused the sheet to fall from her body, revealing a thin slip. I removed the rear seats, putting part of the stretcher on the folded chair next to me. This forced me to climb over her head to get to my seat. As I settled in, her face was inches from my right elbow. I couldn't help but look at her neck. It had been sutured from the autopsy. Brown cord—like used in wrapping packages—zigzagged the closed cut, adding a spooky dimension to this trip. All I needed now was a dark, stormy night with lightning and thunder to have the beginnings of a good horror movie. I wasn't too sure who else would've taken this flight for the $5-an-hour pay. And that was only when the blades were spinning.

As I prepared for takeoff, I pulled the sheet forward, placing my maps on her face. There was no other place to put them. And the crazy thing was that I was so excited to have a paying job I couldn't stand it.

I made the trip to Hope, calling the hearse to pick up the body. When she was gone, I put the stretcher back in and breathed a sigh of relief since there was no face to worry about.

Back at the office, I logged my time and collected my pay. I was an official, real-life, professional pilot.

For the next two years, I flew bodies for that mortician. Always, the face was right next to me. Sometimes I flew a body *from* Fort Worth, and other times I flew to a city and picked up a body. That's how bad I wanted to fly.

I continued through my training, picking up the certifications and licenses in order. When I was legally allowed to give lessons, I did. One day, I went out with a guy who hadn't flown in three years. He needed a refresher. One of the exercises he needed to cover was emergency landings. As we made our approach, the engine quit, providing us with a *real* emergency landing. I put the Cessna 150 down in a farmer's field north of Meacham Field, landing safely before coming to a stop. I tried to get a start on the engine but couldn't. Left with no option, we trudged over to the farmer's house and asked to use their phone.

I called the flight school and the owner answered. I expected him to ask, "Are you all okay?" or "Are you injured?" Instead, the first words out of his mouth were, "Is there any damage to the airplane?"

"No," I told him. "The plane is undamaged." *And thanks for caring.*

He said he'd be right over to check out the plane. A thorough inspection showed it to be in good shape. The problem now was getting it out of the field. High grass and unpredictable ruts made a takeoff iffy, if not downright dangerous. We walked to the end of the proposed runway and found a creek a few feet in front of a barbed-wire fence. High grass. Nasty ruts. A barbed-wire fence. A creek. It seemed like some kind of video game or a scene from an Indiana Jones movie. This was going to be tough.

After studying the terrain, the owner decided it was worth the risk so long as I was the pilot. "You're the lightest," he explained.

He calculated the tiniest amount of fuel needed to take off and fly the few hundred yards to Meacham Field, then drained the rest. When you're desperate for logbook hours, risk looks different.

After revving up the engine to maximum and back down, I released the brake and gripped the wheel, pushing the throttle forward. It was a very bouncy ride as I dodged the ruts, my eyes fixed on the approaching fence. As I reached the absolute last point of departure, where there'd be no way the plane could climb high enough to clear the fence, I pulled the yoke back and rotated the plane up. With a stall warning echoing around the cabin, my landing gear just missed the top strand of wire (they told me later) and I touched down safely at Meacham. I added another two minutes to my logbook—two *torturous* minutes—and another experience to what I hoped would be a long career as an airline pilot.

Texas is a little more conservative than other states when it comes to male-female roles. I didn't realize it at the time, because I wasn't talking to other female pilots. There weren't many to talk to, and we didn't have cell phones or Facebook. The corporate jobs I applied for went to the men because they usually had more hours. During one interview, the hiring manager said, "Well, you've got plenty of experience in the airplane and your flight time is good and everything, but we can't have a girl flying our executives. After all, what would the wives think?"

I was dumbfounded. I didn't care what the wives thought. I just wanted to fly the airplane. Still, I kept applying and interviewing, hoping someone would give me a chance.

I graduated from TCU in 1974 with a degree in Spanish and interior design. People asked me if I was going to decorate airplanes in Mexico. I explained that I had to have a degree to get hired by the big airlines and they didn't care what it was in. Of course, I also minored in Mexican food thanks to Joe T. Garcia's.

Now that I had some serious hours on my logbook, I got a peek at the better jobs. One of them was with the Cohlmia Freight Company. I loved that job. I was their only female pilot, which was kind of a big deal. Five nights a week, I flew freight out of Love Field from nine p.m. until three in the morning. It was the first time I'd been on salary, making $700 per month.

The great thing about this job was a regular schedule and six hours of flight time logged each day. I had to build up my hours if I was going to have a chance. The only downside was the planes. They were horribly neglected.

One night in Oklahoma City, I shot an approach down to our weather minimums and needed the directional gyro to establish a heading. The gyro was spinning like a top. I couldn't even maintain a heading to get established on the guidance to the runway. The controllers had to call out, "Five degrees left… Five more degrees left…" With part of my instruments missing, I made it. I was never so happy in my life to get on the ground. Still, I climbed back in the cockpit and kept going. It was my job.

"So, Tom, did I keep you awake enough to give Duke a break?"

"Did you?" I replied. "I was thoroughly entertained. And I agree that women had a much tougher road, especially in a state like Texas. What you accomplished is incredible!"

"Well, thank you, Tom, but I had a lot of help along the way. Like when I was working for Cohlmia and came down with the flu. Remember that?"

"Of course. You couldn't make it and needed me to fly with you in the copilot's seat. I couldn't believe the beat-up, old airplanes you flew. And those Podunk airports with three-thousand-foot airstrips, all while carrying a load of canceled checks, airplane parts for Rockwell, and Fotomat film. I'm telling you, Beverley, that was some first-class piloting."

"Thanks. And don't forget you did that two nights in a row so I could make it to the weekend and recover. That's a true friend. Although I *was* jealous when we put our resumes in together at American Airlines and you got hired but I didn't. They were the only airline I wanted to fly for because they had the prettiest planes. I was sunk when they turned me down."

"Yeah, Bud Ehmann, the vice president of flight, hired me in July of seventy-six. He said the reason I got the nod over the other applicants was the fact that I had graduated from night school with honors while working all day at the flight school. When I showed him my last two years of making the dean's list, that cinched it. They thought it was something that I could pull that off."

"You had jet time and I had none. You also had important connections like the Quiet Birdmen. I wanted to go to one meeting and see what they were about."

"It's a national fraternal order of pilots—civilian and military—going back to World War Two. They meet once a month, tell stories, and eat dinner. And yes, there is a cash bar."

"You and Big T were members, along with some of the big shots at American. You could've taken me as your date. But you did redeem yourself."

"That's right. I did redeem myself, because Albert Brown, the director of flight training, was a Quiet Birdman. I was in his party group and felt emboldened. One day I went up to the third floor of the flight academy—the Ivory Tower, we called it—and walked in like I was some big shot. Keep in mind I'd heard them talking about how they wanted to hire some women but couldn't find any of them who were qualified. I knew your hours and qualifications backward and forward. You were well-qualified. I knocked on the door and Albert told me to come on in. I asked him why they'd turned you down and if I could see your records. He said the medical records were private, but referred me to the man next door, a doctor. He pulled your file and said you weren't tall enough. You listed five-foot-five and needed to be five-foot-six. I said, 'Why don't we get her measured?'"

"That's what's stupid. I was actually five-six, but because my pilot's license said five-five, I was afraid to put something down that disagreed with my license. When you opened up the door, I went in and they put me on the scale with a telescoping measuring stick. Instead of slouching, I stood upright, squeezing every inch out of my body. They reached down and pulled up my pant legs to see if I was standing on my toes. Sure enough, I made the height and got hired, losing a ton of seniority due to the delay. I would've been the number two woman but for one inch!"

"That had to be a great feeling, being hired at American Airlines."

"It was. You know, from the time I was born, this was my destiny. As a kid, we traveled a lot, so I flew in airplanes—as long as I got the window seat. Just walking out to the airplane in those days and climbing up the rollout stairs and taking in the smells… I loved it.

"I can still remember Page Field in Fort Myers. My mother would go to this machine and buy flight insurance. One year, my mom and I flew to New York because she wanted me to see the snow. Dad couldn't get away from work, so we left him at home. The next morning, we woke up and learned that a United Airlines and TWA airplane had collided over New York City. One hundred and twenty-eight people were killed. Dad refused to let us fly back home, making us take the train instead. Despite the air disaster and the long trip home, my enthusiasm to fly remained strong. I guess I was born with struts for bones and hydraulic fluid for blood."

"That's for sure," I said.

"Tom, tell Duke about your 9/11 experience."

"Yeah, that was frightening. Flying a plane to New York on 9/11. But really, the only pilot I know who has a fascinating 9/11 story is you, Beverley. Why don't you tell Duke what happened with your flight?"

I looked at the first mate's chair and it was empty. Rubbing my eyes, I checked it again. *Where did she go? She was just there.*

I ducked my head and searched the salt-caked windscreen for an opening. I found one and located Venus. Sure enough, I was still headed east.

Glancing down at my Croc, I noticed the hole was slightly bigger. Duke was doing his job.

I checked the empty chair for Beverley one more time. *I sure enjoyed her company.*

A loneliness I hadn't felt before caked my heart. I hoped I could complete my mission and see Beverley one more time.

Chapter Ten

When I landed a job at American Airlines, I'd been working for Shenandoah, racking up time in their Learjet. Shenandoah had been paying for my flight training so I could get a captain's rating on the Learjet. Because they'd been so good to me, I didn't have the heart to take any more of their money, get the rating, then leave. Instead, I left those hours behind along with great relationships. It was worth it.

American Airlines sent me to their training academy in Fort Worth, right across the street from Euless—home of Big T's dwindling empire. Even though I still lived with my parents, out-of-town trainees stayed at the Western Hills Inn. This kept the Caribe Club full and the liquor bottles empty.

When we needed to climb in a real jet, that happened at the Great Southwest Airport. It was a mile away from the training academy. With book work one day and actual flying the next, the training was excellent.

During the eight-week program, I received $750 a month. That wasn't much, especially for the pilots who didn't live with their parents.

With my extensive experience, I breezed through the training. At graduation, they assigned me to New York and put me in a Boeing 727 as a flight engineer. It was a great place to start.

There's more to being a flight engineer than one might think. I sat in a third seat behind the copilot, facing a systems panel on the starboard side of the plane. My job was to run all the preflight checks and operate that panel. On takeoff, I set the power after the captain advanced the throttles. In the air, I operated the electrical, fuel, and hydraulics of the aircraft, while constantly watching for problems. If an emergency popped up, I had the spotlight, reacting to save the plane. In some respects, it seemed more like a supervisory role. But it wasn't. I was a junior officer, not even considered a pilot.

The great part of being a flight engineer was how much I learned. I had the best seat on the plane to observe the pilots flying.

I moved to New York and quickly discovered that $750 a month didn't go far. American had told me during training that they intentionally paid this amount for twelve months. This low wage strategy accomplished four goals. First, it sorted out the ones who didn't want it. I'd have to survive like this for one full year before I could be bumped up to real pay. Second, the airlines saved money. The bean counters loved that. Third, once I was making good money, they wanted me to think long and hard about quitting. Another airline would probably put me through another year of starvation wages. This swung the financial calculation in favor of staying at American Airlines. And finally, the company's worst-case scenario was paying me a great wage, training me, and then watching me walk out the door at the end of that training to go to a competitor. A low wage minimized the damage if that happened.

The only way I could live in New York with that salary was to stay with another pilot. We split the costs of an apartment. Since we were gone most of the time, it worked out.

Around the time I was hired, men wanted to be stewardesses. The airlines didn't want to call them stewards, and they certainly couldn't call them stewardesses. To solve this problem, they came up with the generic term "flight attendant." At the same time, the nomenclature of pilot and copilot changed to captain and first officer. And as plane design changed, they did away with the flight engineers on all aircraft except the very large ones. This saved a big salary, which, again, was something the bean counters loved.

Living in New York wasn't much fun to me. It was just an expensive, not to mention rude, welcome to this born-and-raised Fort Worth boy. No way it was the Big Apple. More like a Cactus Pear—something I wanted to avoid.

After a short time, I decided to put in a transfer to DFW. I wanted to go home.

Personnel transferred me to Chicago instead of Dallas. I leased an apartment and had been there for one month when my transfer to DFW came through. The landlord graciously let me out of my lease. I moved back into my parents' house just as Beverley completed training and moved to New York. In a month or so, Beverley and my buddies were on the phone telling me how much fun they were having in New York. I'm sure someone in personnel thought I was a mental case when I asked to be transferred *back* to New York. Due to the low pay we received, New York always had plenty of openings. I received the transfer quickly.

When I arrived in New York, I discovered that Beverley was dating another man. I was crushed. Even though I'd been dating some flight attendants, I considered her my girl. I guess I should have checked with her first. From what I learned, she was happy with this guy and apparently over me. This forced me to move on.

I flew home often to savor the taste of Texas. My parents still lived in their old house. Dad was hanging on to his Big T image. But with his business declining, he was more like Little T. His girlfriend/secretary, Marilyn, refused a prosthetic, instead wearing her arm in a sling for the rest of her life. And Mom continued ignoring Marilyn's presence.

It was nice to see my parents for a few days and nice to leave. I was no longer a kid. I had left the nest for good, and this changed our relationship from one of parent-child to friends-with-baggage.

In New York, I managed to find a high-rise apartment I could share with another flight engineer. He was from New Hampshire and easy to get along with. Again, we were gone so often we usually had the place to ourselves.

At the six-month mark, American Airlines bumped me up twenty-five dollars a month. The extra pay was a joke. If I hadn't had some savings to fall back on, it would've been rough.

I started dating more flight attendants. They seemed to like a man in a uniform, even if I wasn't yet a first officer or captain. On one flight from New York to Dallas, I met Donna Ryan. She had just completed training and was on reserve when American called her in to work for another flight attendant who'd missed her connection. I got to talking with her, especially when we turned around and flew back to New York. We landed at Kennedy then did a Providence, Rhode Island turnaround. By the time our day was over, I was interested.

Donna was twenty-two and I was twenty-five. With our crazy schedules, we continued dating when we could see each other. She was extremely pretty and very fun-loving. She enjoyed traveling and wanted to see the world. And she was full of energy. That excited me.

Each time we were together, I felt more excitement. By 1979, we'd been dating two years and had both transferred to Dallas. I was also bumped up to copilot, or first officer. That brought more pay.

Donna gave notice to American Airlines and quit shortly after arriving in Dallas. Her father and mine put together some financing and helped set her up in the trucking business. She even rented an apartment in one of Big T's fourplexes.

A year later, I was over at her apartment when she suggested we should plan a vacation. I said, "Well, if you really want to plan something, why don't you plan our honeymoon?" I didn't have a ring or any plan. I just blurted it out. It wasn't very romantic, but it worked. We had a nice wedding, and all of a sudden, we were married. I felt like the luckiest guy in the world.

Donna worked hard to know my parents. It didn't take long before they absolutely adored her. She and my mother were best friends. I liked her parents, but they were in Detroit. I didn't see them much.

In 1981—two years after working the trucking business—Donna closed it down. Her father, who also had a trucking business, sent some drivers down to take the trucks back to Detroit. Donna was always a hard worker and found a spot managing a chain of dry cleaners for a good friend of my parents. She managed a store for two years before buying her own store in Colleyville.

In 1983, I became a captain. With Donna's store and my large paycheck, we were doing well. We were young and had money, so we traveled all over the world. We went with my parents on many trips. It was a special time in our lives.

For my thirtieth birthday party, Donna rented out a nightclub. Near the end of the party, a large cake was wheeled in and a topless stripper popped out to dance with me. Donna was always great about picking out special birthday gifts. For one birthday, she gave me a Rolex watch. For my next birthday, she had it refitted with a diamond bezel. And in 1985, she gave me a special birthday gift—a neckchain with a crucifix, a ship's wheel, and a ship's anchor, along with keys to a boat. It was a 36-foot Trojan sport fishing motor yacht docked one hour north of DFW on Lake Texoma. I named it the *Prima D*. It was incredible.

I began driving to the lake as soon as I was done flying for the week. Because I'd joined the airlines right before a large hiring spree, I was very senior even though I was a new captain. I got my schedule to where I'd fly hard for three days and have four off. On Thursday, I'd jump in my car and head to the lake where I'd party with the other boaters until Donna could join me Saturday evening. She'd have fun and we'd come back Sunday. Then we'd start the week all over again. This went on for years.

Later in our marriage, she had several miscarriages. This devastated both of us. I sold the boat she had bought me and purchased a forty-three-foot Hatteras motor yacht. She still came to the lake every weekend until 1996, when our marriage started to crumble. We were both stubborn and argued a lot. Of course, I kept going to the lake and partied harder than ever. This didn't help matters.

In 1998, the dry-cleaning chain along with Donna's store were bought up by an investor. When she told me she wanted a divorce, it wasn't a complete shock. But I fought it all the way. It was one of the few times I couldn't talk her out of something. It was like Big T used to say, "A woman's faults are few. Men only have two: everything they say and everything they do." Guilty as charged.

Here I was, forty-six years old, alone, and single again. I didn't know what to do.

A sharp pain shot up from my Big Toe. I took my eyes off the rolling ocean and saw Duke biting me.

"Okay, boy, I'm awake. I may have faded back there a bit, but I'm alert now."

He turned away and sauntered over to the first mate's chair. He sniffed at a smooth tanned leg and licked it.

"Thanks, Duke. I always figured you liked me better."

"Donna!" I cried, seeing her sitting there in a white cotton blouse, shorts, and sandals. "What are you doing here?"

She brushed back her hair. "You named the boat after me. Remember? The *Prima D*? The least I could do was make sure you got it to shore in one piece."

"Gosh, am I glad to see you. I'm down to one engine and bad off. I need to stay awake to keep the boat pointed in the right direction."

"Well, Tom, I stayed up many a night on Lake Texoma. I guess I can keep you up while we reminisce on old times. But you sure glossed over everything—our first date, our wedding, and our trips. What about our marriage? We were married almost twenty years. Can't you do a little better than that?"

"Actually, my voice is getting hoarse talking to Duke. Can you talk for a while?"

The corners of her mouth turned up. "I sure can, but do you mind me starting at the beginning?"

"Honey, I'm so glad to see you, you can start wherever you want."

"Okay," she said, straightening her blouse. "Now pay attention, Duke. Here goes."

Chapter Eleven

When I first met your daddy, I was a reserve flight attendant. Being a "reserve" meant that I was on call for four-to-five-day stretches. I had certain days off each month, but otherwise, I sat by the phone waiting to be called in to replace other flight attendants who were sick, missed connections, or didn't show up. When the call came, I had to be at one of three different airports within two hours. With New York City traffic, that was a tall order. Usually, though, I made it with fifteen minutes to spare.

Living in New York—Manhattan, actually—wasn't bad, except for the snow. Tom was a flight engineer, the first person I'd see when I entered the cockpit. He was cute with a nice smile. But I was engaged to a guy back in Detroit. As I got to talking with Tom, I said to myself, *That guy in Detroit is trouble. To heck with him. I'm going to try something different.* I asked Tom out and he said yes.

We went to a place called Paxton's in Midtown Manhattan. It was set up like a diner, but was a bar/restaurant. We had fun and I felt a good connection.

Because both of us had different schedules, we continued dating casually. He was seeing other people too. But within six months, we were serious. Still, other than that initial flight, I never worked another one with Tom.

Tom was a city boy with country experience. I was mostly a suburb girl who'd grown up in Farmington, Michigan. Mom was a stay-at-home housewife and Dad had a local cartage company within the Detroit area. I was the oldest of three sisters and one brother. I was more in charge and the boss of the family back then. With Tom and me both being first-borns, we butted heads later on.

I went through high school and worked for Dad's trucking company while I attended night school. When I graduated in 1976, I applied to American, was accepted, and started in 1977. It was time for me to move on and experience something different. Being a flight attendant allowed me to see the world.

They trained me in Dallas and automatically sent me to the New York area. I was twenty-two and full of energy. It was an exciting adventure.

As we continued to date, we became exclusive. When Tom transferred back to Dallas, I put in my own request and followed him several months later. By now, we'd been dating close to two years.

Although I appreciated the job with American, I hated the uncertainty of vacations and spending time with my family. The more I got to know Tom's family, the more I grew comfortable turning in my notice and trying the trucking business.

The big idea was to operate a hot shot trucking business out of Irving. My trucks would make same-day deliveries to businesses that needed parts right away. My father helped with the trucks and advice, and both he and Tom's father helped with financing.

Almost as soon as I started, diesel prices rose. This crushed business, because the cost of delivering one or two items forced the customers to think twice about how badly they needed it. With no consolidation facility, we just weren't making any money. Two years after I started, I closed the business.

Tom and I got married, and yes, it was less than a romantic proposal. But the wedding was first-class. We held it at the First Baptist Church in Euless, with a reception at Woodhaven Country Club in Fort Worth. We had a cute photo taken on the golf course of Tom putting while I stood behind him with my hands on my hips. At the rehearsal dinner, Big T even stood up and gave a speech. He turned to me and said, "I'm glad you've got him now, because I don't want him back."

I married Tom because I had a great deal of respect for him. I admired and loved him. We were very compatible.

We went to my parents' getaway place in Winterhaven, Florida, after the wedding. Then we took a week-long honeymoon cruise through the Southern Caribbean before it was back to work as a married couple.

Things started out good, and they were good for a long time. Tom was two and a half years older than me and we were both headstrong, neither one flexible. At times, he was a bully. I thought it would go away or I'd learn to deal with it. There were cracks, but it was a good, solid marriage. We trusted each other and worked to build something together.

With my trucking business over, I moved into the dry-cleaning business. The Putts, good friends of Tom's parents, had a chain of Town and Country dry cleaners. I managed the Trophy Club store and eleven others for two years before partnering with the Putts on my own store in Colleyville. I had a dry-cleaning plant, but sent all the laundry to one of two plants the Putts had. Dealing with laundry is mostly a break-even affair in the cleaning business. All the profit is in the dry-cleaning. Laundry is taken in to get to the customers' dry cleaning.

When an employee didn't show up, I'd have to take over and press the clothes. Sometimes Tom came from home and helped. But with his bad back and previous injuries from playing football and falling on an airport conveyor, it was hard for Tom to always be there. At least he had the best uniforms.

For Tom's birthdays, I always tried to give him something special. I had friends help pick out the boat. I bought it from the Grandpappy Point Marina. That was the biggest gift of all.

His parents usually came to the birthday parties. I truly loved them. It was like I had two sets of parents. They treated me like a daughter.

Helen, Tom's mother, and I ran around together. When I say we were best friends, I mean *best* friends. She never talked about her husband's other woman unless I got her drinking. Then she'd admit there was something there but claim it had been over a long time ago. I only saw Big T's girlfriend once, by accident. I never pushed the issue.

With both of us making good money, Tom and I bought a beautiful home in Trophy Club. We traveled all the time, taking Big Trips to Australia, New Zealand, Europe, the South Pacific, and a private yacht in the Greek Isles. We had the good life.

When Tom bought the bigger boat, I stopped coming to the lake. It was a grind. I would finish up with the store by two, then go home and load up the dogs, overnight bag, and food. I would drive at least an hour and park. Then I would haul everything from the car to the boat. That night, I would have fun. The next morning, I got up and cleaned the inside of the boat while Tom cleaned the outside. We would haul everything back to the car, load up the dogs, and drive back home, where I unloaded it all. I would relax for a few hours, go to bed, and get up Monday morning to hit it all over again. So yeah, I stopped coming. This meant we saw each other less.

In 1998, Town and Country Cleaners was bought out by a small family of investors. That's when I asked Tom for a divorce. There were a lot of factors at play.

We had tried to have children with in vitro for two to three years and had suffered five miscarriages. Because we started when I was thirty-nine, I was a high-risk pregnancy. Tom pointed a lot of fingers at me. I worked around all that steam and chemicals. The arguments over not being able to have children were symptoms of a problem.

We both had tempers, but I was disciplined with alcohol. Tom's father always had a drink in his hand. My parents maybe had a drink on New Year's Eve, so I'd never gotten used to drinking. Unfortunately, Tom's drinking brought out his anger toward his father and led to him bullying me. I couldn't take it any longer. It was sad.

Tom didn't take it well, and neither did I. There are always two sides to a divorce, so I can't lay the blame solely on him.

That wouldn't be fair. And, like Tom, I was disappointed our marriage failed.

When you go through something like that, you discover the hidden phases of the process. The first is when one spouse asks the other for a divorce. This brings out a lot of emotions like anger, resentment, bitterness, and resistance. Once you get through that, the serving of the papers comes next. This causes the previous emotions to erupt again. When it's final, there's profound sadness and depression over a failed relationship. Neither spouse ever thought they'd be divorced. Now, they are.

With the marriage over, the next phase is when one of the parties begins dating. The other spouse feels inadequate or left out. When a relationship turns serious, the other spouse is bitter, maybe even jealous. That happened with us.

After my divorce, I took some time off before working again. I had known Bob through a golfing event while I was separated. He asked me out. I pushed him off until I finally said yes. Tom found out about it and was quite angry. It took two years before he came around. Eventually, he and I became friends again and he respected Bob. When Bob and I married, that was the final divorce stage. It's like a final exclamation point in the failed marriage. There's no going back. Is that right, Tom?

"Huh?" I said.

"Were you napping, not listening to anything I said?" Donna asked with a frown.

"No, I heard you. I just wish we'd tried harder. I know I was a bully and drank too much. I guess I get upset because I screwed up the best thing I ever had."

"We had some great years. There's no denying it." Donna leaned back and laughed. "I forgot about the time I worked a flight and met the girl before me—Beverley Bass. She was a gorgeous blonde you seemed to be fond of."

"She was. I've had more than one woman break my heart. But after twenty years, yours hurt the worst."

Donna smiled uneasily. "I was hurting too. It was so bad I put together a girls' trip to cheer me up. Remember? Helen and my mother, along with my sister, flew to New York and took the Cunard *QE2* to England. There, we took the Orient Express up to London, stayed for a while, and flew back on the Concord. It was something I needed. And your mother was good for me."

I cracked a laugh. "Yeah, who's ever heard of an ex-spouse hanging out with her ex-mother-in-law?"

"Helen was never ex anything to me. But now, you're such good friends with Bob, he has a name for you."

"What are you talking about?" I asked.

"You're over at our house so much, I heard Bob telling his friend they couldn't play golf because he has to spend time with his ex-husband-in-law."

"What?!" I said. "I'm an ex-husband-in-law?"

"It's an affectionate term. You know that."

I gripped the wheel as deep fatigue set in. "Listen, Donna, I know I messed up, but I want you to know that even if I don't make it to land, you're the best thing that ever happened to me. The fact that you loved my parents so much was icing on the cake. It's just that my role model for being a good husband was flawed. I could have done better, yet I didn't. It's a failure I live with every day. And I want you to know I'm so grateful you're still in my life. Bob too. I don't know what I would've done if you'd cut me off completely. You're all I have left of a life lived imperfectly."

My eyes glistened as I wiped them with my shirt. I glanced over at my beautiful ex-wife and she was gone. It was the second time I'd lost her. And the hurt came flooding back.

"You know, Duke," I said, staring down at my faithful companion, "this necklace she gave me, with the anchor, crucifix, and ship's wheel, has gotten me out of a lot of jams. But I'm pretty sure it's the crucifix that has the real power. We just need one final push and we'll reach land. Can you keep me awake for a few more hours?"

He nudged my shin.

"That's what I thought. Now I'll tell you about the rest of my life before you came along."

Chapter Twelve

The wind picked up, howling like a wolf. I had thought this was over, but I was wrong. It might be coming back.

As I looked over at my buddy, his eyes stared back at mine. So, Duke, I don't think I told you that Big T was a great pilot. He was one of the original members of the Admirals Club. They loved him.

Not only was Big T captain in the air, but he was a captain of the seas with a sailing certification. Some people are natural athletes or artists or interior designers. Big T was a natural captain.

It was Easter weekend in 1992 when he decided to travel to the French side of St. Maarten. His best friend and three other buddies had chartered a sailboat. Big T was going to captain it around the Caribbean. He couldn't wait to see what the islands had to offer.

The group of five met up at a popular restaurant, enjoying drinks and a nice meal. As they walked back to the hotel, Big T collapsed to the ground, dying on the spot. A massive heart attack was the cause. I received the news and hung my head. Not only was I crushed, but I knew I had a Big Task ahead of me in bringing Dad home.

St. Maarten and I had some history. Several years before Dad's death, I was the first officer of a DC-10, having been bumped down on the new equipment. We arrived in St. Maarten on a scheduled flight. I spent an uneventful night before waking up to breakfast and another flight out. As I lifted my kit bag up into the cockpit, I threw out my back. It was so bad I couldn't walk.

The captain pulled me aside and said, "We need to get you to a doctor."

"I agree," I told him, "but I don't want it to be in this place."

I had heard from other crews that getting sick on this island was bad news. There was no way I wanted to see a doctor here. And we had 300 passengers. They didn't want to stay on that island any more than I did.

I told the captain, "If you can get me in the seat before the passengers get on, I'll fly home. After all the passengers get off, get me out of the seat and have Special Services meet me at the airplane to get me up the Jetway and into the ramp area. My wife will be there to pick me up."

He frowned, contemplating the matter. "Okay."

They placed me in the right seat, stuffing a pillow behind my back and leaning the chair toward the flight engineer. Between them, they got the plane home, because I wasn't worth a rock on that flight. It was one of the only times I can remember feeling out of control on a flight.

Needless to say, I didn't have a great attitude when it came to St. Maarten. Now, my father had died there. With no choice, I put off mourning and began the process of bringing his body to Dallas.

I made some calls and got nowhere. We wanted to have an open casket. With day after day slipping by and nothing resolved, that was looking grim.

I learned that two issues were holding up the release of his body. First, the State Department had to issue a "Report of Death of an American Citizen Abroad." They couldn't issue that because money was owed to the funeral home and the doctor who'd pronounced the death. I spend a lot of time tracking that down and discovered the local doctor wanted $60 for putting his stethoscope to Dad's chest and filling out a form. That seemed fair. But then the funeral home decided they'd won the lottery. They asked for $4,007 for holding his body for four days. And this was in 1992!

Since the funeral home did not have the ability to embalm a body, they knew that every day we waited the bill grew higher and the chance of an open casket grew dimmer. We had no choice but to send the money to the bandits.

With the extortion paid, I used my pull to get Dad in the belly of an American Airline DC-10 and back home. Normally, when a body is delivered from overseas, it's taken to the cargo facility nearby where the loved ones can claim it. For Big T, I was able to engage American Airlines' Special Services Department. They promised to make sure Big T received extra-special care.

As the plane came to a stop, Gary and I went down to the ramp to oversee the removal of Big T's casket from the cargo hold. The airport allowed the hearse to pull up next to the cargo hold so the casket could be loaded in. This saved us from having to pick up Dad at the cargo facility.

During this process, the crew held the passengers from deplaning until the body was off. They watched through the windows as Gary and I kissed the casket and a worker placed a small American flag over it. Several baggage claim workers were vets and saluted the casket as it went into the hearse. The DFW police escorted it out of the airport, before the Grapevine police picked it up and escorted it all the way to Mount Olive Funeral Home in Fort Worth.

Once we caught our breath, we had to pay the funeral home to make the body presentable for an open casket, since it hadn't been embalmed. Apparently, $4,007 only went so far in St. Maarten.

At the funeral, servicemen were present to fold the flag draped over the coffin. Marilyn Crenshaw wasn't there. That gave me a little bit of joy. After a colorful life, Big T was buried in Greenwood Cemetery and that was that.

Mom took it surprisingly well, but Gary had a hard time. I hurt too. It was a tough time for the Toler sons.

Flying for American Airlines was a great experience. I was never laid off or furloughed like other airlines experienced. Considering all the crap jobs I'd taken to get airtime in my logbook, the company was truly first class.

They moved me up to captain on January 27, 1987. This promotion put me where I loved to be: in control. I flew Boeings 757 and 767.

As a captain, I had to attend ground school twice a year—one more than as a first officer. At ground school, I received information on new problems that had popped up since the last training. We also brushed up on company procedures. This training lasted four or five days, never more than a week.

Once a year, I had a check ride. Early on in my career, this meant hopping in a plane and taking off. As the simulators became more sophisticated and added real movement, we skipped the actual plane. The realism was unbelievable.

Eventually, American Airlines purchased new planes like the MD-80 and MD-82. For me to fly those, I had to be updated on the new features and "systems differences" as well as do a check ride. Again, early on, this meant a real flight. Later, the simulator was good enough. New plane training lasted four to six weeks.

With the biannual training and the four-to-six-week new-plane training, American put a lot of money into making sure we knew what we were doing. The cost was high. Each day we spent in training was a day we weren't flying. They understood that the money they spent on training was nothing compared to the life-cost of one crash. It wasn't just a number calculation.

One example of all this was when a Delta jet crashed a mile short of DFW Airport. The plane had found itself in a microburst, plummeting to Earth and slamming into a car and two water tanks. Only 28 of the 165 on board survived. The FAA created a program for us to learn how to escape a downburst in any airplane. That's the way it was with plane crashes. Once an investigation was complete, the recommendations automatically became part of our training at the next six-month checkup. Between American Airlines and the FAA, we had a thorough and complete training program.

I remember it was a sunny Friday. I was enjoying an off day when I received a call from one of the chief pilots. He said they had selected me and two other captains to fly President Clinton from Washington to Las Vegas, and then from Las Vegas to the San Francisco area. President Clinton was combining work with a reelection tour.

"Will you do it?" the chief pilot asked.

"Well, sure," I said, wondering how many pilots had turned them down. He assured me that a crew would call and give me all the particulars.

It turned out I had been assigned to fly the initial leg. I couldn't fly the entire route due to a restriction on the amount of time a pilot can fly. I, my copilot, and one American Airline representative flew an empty Boeing 757 into Andrews Air Force Base. The Boeing 757 came in two versions—a single-aisle or double-aisle. I flew the single-aisle Boeing with three seats on either side. This version is the most common.

Before I made this trip, I learned that union rules required the most senior pilots who were available to fly charter flights like this. Two pilots who were available were senior to me but had been passed over by the chief pilot. Under the rules, those pilots had to be paid the same as I was. American picked up the tab for that. Like Beverley said, I had a lot of connections.

A lieutenant colonel picked us up and took us to a hotel across the street from the base. The next morning, they came and collected us. We checked out the plane while they loaded the airplane with the White House china and other accoutrements. Our mission was to fly the White House travel staff and the rest of the press corps. Air Force One has only so many seats allocated for the press corps. The leftovers were on my aircraft. This arrangement always necessitated a charter like ours or a military aircraft to haul everyone else.

Before the flight, my first officer did the walkaround while I completed the flight plan and verified the fuel load. As captain, I was the only one who could sign for the fuel. With that done, we were ready to go.

We were the lead aircraft to Las Vegas. Our job was to clear the air space for the President. Our plane's designation was Air Force One, even though the President and the real Air Force One were thirty minutes behind us. The President's Air Force One is flown by military pilots with the Air Force. The captain is usually a full colonel and the first officer a lieutenant colonel.

Not only were we clearing out the airspace, but we had to get there first so the press could set up the cameras to catch the moment the President emerged from the plane. We had to speed up or slow down depending on the location of the President's plane.

The flight was easy and uneventful. Maybe one of the reporters dropped a fork or something. That was it. In Las Vegas, I handed the plane over to another pilot and flew back to Dallas with two ball caps, one that said Andrews Air Force Base—Home of Air Force One, and the other with the golf course of St. Andrews on the sides and the presidential seal on the front.

Besides flying ahead for the President, I occasionally had celebrities on board. When I flew the Jet Commander for the Wortham Brothers, I enjoyed the company of Roy Rogers and Dale Evans. They were pleasant and kind. Then there was Jimmy Stewart when I flew for Shenandoah. When I flew for American Airlines, I had an interesting flight involving Dottie West and the Gatlin Brothers. They had flown from Los Angeles to Dallas with another crew and were still seated in the plane at the gate. The plane was continuing on to Nashville but had a two-hour layover in Dallas. This was where problems occurred.

The previous crew asked the passengers who were continuing on to Nashville to deplane. Corporate rules stated a pilot could not leave passengers on board without at least a flight attendant present. Yet this crew had been flying for a while and had to catch another flight or go home. When the flight attendant explained this to the celebrities, they were upset. Dottie West, though, worked herself into a tizzy. I heard alcohol was likely involved.

The Gatlin Brothers understood and left the plane. But Dottie West wanted to argue some more. Eventually, they coaxed her off the plane and into the gate area. This was where I came into the picture.

Like usual, I arrived and began checking out the aircraft. Before I could get down the Jetway, a flight attendant told me Dottie West was still upset. She started complaining to another flight attendant and this kicked the problem up to me. I spoke to her and explained how things worked. I think she was just grumpy from flying a lot. I checked the plane out, and before long, Dottie was back in first class and happy again.

Besides spending a lot of money on training us, American invested in maintaining the aircraft. I rarely had any problems. I never lost an engine or had to make an emergency landing. The training and maintenance kept us flying. If a plane did have a problem, it was quickly pulled from service and repaired. At American Airlines, everything went smoothly.

The closest I came to a plane crash was at the 1977 Paris Air Show. I was in the stands when an A-10 Warthog crashed. They had a fairly low ceiling that day—about 3,000 feet—and the pilot tried to keep his loops within the confines of the ceiling. He stalled it on the bottom end, hitting the runway real hard and separating the cockpit from the titanium fuselage. He died on the way to the hospital. Unfortunately, I saw that up front and personal.

A certain comedian highly recommends that whatever happens in life, don't let your worlds collide. I think any guy, when it comes to the women in his life—past and present—wants to keep them separate. No sense in allowing them to compare notes.

One afternoon, I was picking Donna up at the DFW Airport when I saw her walking off the plane with Beverley Bass. They were talking and laughing like long-lost friends. The two gorgeous blondes, one my former girlfriend and the other my current girlfriend, seemed hellbent on making me squirm. Mission: Accomplished!

I learned later that Donna had been working the flight with Beverley as the first officer. What were the odds?

Donna had a Cheshire cat smile stretched across her face as I drove her back to Big T's fourplex. Needless to say, I received a great deal of teasing. And I never did find out what they talked about.

I had acquaintances, but not many close buddies. One great friend, however, was Chip Moody. I was in my early twenties working at the flight school one Sunday morning when in walked a familiar face—Chip. He was seven years older than me and news anchor on DFW's Channel Five. He was like a celebrity to me.

"I'd like to learn to fly," he said.

"I can handle that," I told him. And those words were the beginning of a long friendship.

We spent a lot of time together, getting to know each other's wives. If I was off, I'd go watch one of his newscasts. When he worked for WFAA Channel 8, he was part of a powerhouse lineup. Chip Moody (news anchor), Tracy Rowlett (co-anchor), Dale Hansen (sports), and Troy Dungan (weather). They dominated the ratings. And he had the television look.

Afterward, we might head to Miller's Pub, a place where all the newsmen and women congregated. Sometimes we took in a Mavericks game, leaving early so he could make the broadcast. He and his wife also came to Lake Texoma one time to hang out on our boat. But Chip didn't care for boating.

One story shows how close we were. Chip decided he wanted to go to St. Maarten's island. I was recently divorced from Donna. "Why don't you grab a girl and meet me there?" he said.

I agreed and flew to the island a couple days ahead of him. I managed to get a room in the same hotel the American Airline crews stayed. It was next to the airport, right on the beach. After I checked into the hotel with my girl, I said to her, "I'm going back to the airport to rent a car. Then we can cruise around the island and see some sights."

When I got back, I discovered she was on the beach. I waved to her from the balcony. She saw me and headed back to the room. As soon as she closed the door, she said, "You need to call Chip."

"Why? What's going on? Is he not coming or what?"

She shook her head. "You just need to call Chip."

I called the news station, and the first person I talked to was Troy Dungan, the weatherman. "Tom, have you talked to Chip yet?"

"No," I said, wondering what was going on. I couldn't tell if someone had died or they were pulling a prank on me.

"Why don't I just let Chip give you the news," Troy said, passing the phone to Chip.

I waited a few seconds before finally hearing my good friend's voice. "Tom, what's the first thing you told me to do when you were teaching me to be a pilot?"

"That's easy. Check the weather."

He chuckled. "Well, you crazy bastard, haven't you checked the weather? Don't you know there's a hurricane coming your way?"

"No, I didn't know that."

"Let me put you back on the line with Troy."

Troy gave me the bad news. Sure enough, it was a big one headed straight toward St. Maarten's. Embarrassingly, I'd been oblivious to it.

I hung up and immediately called American Airlines dispatch. "What's the deal with the hurricane? Can you get me out of here?"

"It's a bad one. If you can get off the island now, I suggest you do so. We're about to pull the airplanes out of there. Once we do that, there aren't going to be any airplanes back in there for at least two weeks."

I couldn't believe it. How had I let this happen?

My girl and I went back to the airport, turned the rental car in, and found a line snaking out the terminal and around the building.

I knew I wouldn't have any problem getting out because as a crew member, I could fly on the jump seat in the cockpit. But my girlfriend? Well, I sure was going to miss her.

As fate would have it, I knew the captain of the second-to-last flight off the island. They had an empty flight attendant jump seat for my girlfriend. It wasn't allowed per regulations, but he was retiring in two days. "What are they going to do?" he said with a shrug. "Fire me?"

Incredibly, my girlfriend and I made the flight. However, it was going to Puerto Rico. We stayed one night there. The next morning, I knew the captain of the flight leaving for Dallas and did the same thing. We got out of there before the hurricane hit. What a disaster that would've been.

I really enjoyed my friendship with Chip. But it wasn't a shock when he died in 2001 from Hodgkin's disease. He had been fighting it for years. And one day after Christmas, too. He was only fifty-four. Much too young for such a great guy and consummate professional.

As I said, American Airlines was easy to fly for. I did, however, have one flight that was somewhat eventful. We were the second flight scheduled to take off from the DFW Airport for LaGuardia at 8:01 a.m. Each morning, a slate of planes took off for the eastern seaboard—Boston, Washington, D.C., Philadelphia, Baltimore, and New York. My plane was crammed full of passengers and jet fuel. As fate would have it, we happened to be the first of the eastbound planes to pull back.

I taxied to the runway and received clearance to take off. Advancing the throttles up to 80 knots, I headed down the runway and heard a voice in my headset. "American 708. DFW Tower. Cancel takeoff clearance."

I glanced at my copilot to make sure I'd heard that, then aborted the takeoff.

The tower had me immediately get back in line, which was very strange. I asked for some information and they said, "A small airplane has hit one of the World Trade Center Towers."

I informed the crew and passengers of the delay and told them we were waiting for further instructions. A few minutes later, the flight attendants buzzed me. "Some of the passengers have AM radios and they're listening to the news. It's a not a small plane but a commercial jet like ours. One passenger said it *was* ours."

"Okay," I said. "We're trying to find out now."

Back in line, we had four planes in front of us and five planes to the rear. As we idled in line, my ACARS printer dinged. I looked down and saw a roll of paper spitting up. I pulled on it so I could read the words. "Captain Toler. There is a POSITIVE SABOTAGE THREAT on board. Return to the gate as soon as possible."

A "positive sabotage threat" told me I had a bomb on board. I read the rest of the message. "Do not respond on the radio. It's being monitored. Call dispatch from the gate using a landline phone."

Instantly, my heart took off. I had a ticking time bomb on board, yet I was stuck in line. Like an Alfred Hitchcock movie, there was nowhere to go.

I contacted the control tower but couldn't tell them my problem. I searched for words to convey the urgency of the situation but stumbled over them. It was maddening.

"Uh, DFW Tower. America 708. I've got a mechanical problem. You need to let me return to the gate now."

"American 708. What kind of mechanical problem?"

"It's a problem that requires my immediate return to the gate."

"Can't you wait until the planes ahead clear?"

"Negative. I must return now."

After several back and forth conversations like that, they managed to get everybody out of the way. They put some on the runway and put others on a parallel taxiway. I taxied to the nearest perpendicular taxiway and drove to the ramp fast. But I needed to tell the passengers something, especially if the bomber was on board.

"Folks, this is the captain speaking. We have a mechanical problem—a red light on the control panel. We need to get it checked out back at the ramp. Sorry for the delay. I'll need you to deplane when we reach the gate."

Now I had another problem. "American 708. Ramp Control. The gates are completely full."

"Sir," I said forcefully, "we have a mechanical problem and need to get the passengers off this plane."

This was bad. The bomber could easily see that I was trying to pull into a gate and let the passengers off. If he was able, he could detonate it now. If the bomb had a timer, every second meant we were that much closer to an explosion. If by chance the bomb had an altitude sensor exploding the plane at 20,000 feet, then we were safe. I pondered the possibilities.

Triggering a bomb remotely would mean the bomber had to be on board and use a wireless device. If so, he was ready to die for his cause. It was likely on a timer, but I hoped for an altitude sensor.

The flight attendant buzzed me and said, "Captain, we just heard from a passenger that another commercial jet has flown into the second tower."

This wasn't going to be an ordinary day. There was no way I was flying this plane anywhere. I had to get my crew and passengers off now!

I clicked on the radio. "Ramp Control. This is American 708. You have five minutes to open a gate or I am deploying the slides. Then you guys can worry about how you're going to get the passengers up to the terminal because they're going to be out there walking around on the ramp."

That did it. They backed out a plane that had not started boarding to make room for us. I pulled my plane in and slammed on the brakes. We hustled the passengers off, letting them take their carry-ons. What the authorities did with the passengers, I have no idea.

Once everyone was off, I raced to a bank of pay phones in the gate area and told them the aircraft was clear.

"Captain Toler," they said, "we need to clear the airplane before we send the dogs on board. Make sure the plane is completely empty."

I had to go back onto the plane—the one with the ticking time bomb—and search the lavatories, under the seats, anywhere a person could hide. I verified that the plane was clear and called dispatch.

"Okay, Captain. You can go home."

Just as I hung up the phone, the dogs arrived and headed down the Jetway. I couldn't get out of there fast enough.

I drove straight to my mother's house and found her watching the news. She was crying, and relieved to see me. "They said an American Airlines jet crashed into the north tower and I thought it was you."

I hugged her until she was comforted. By this time, two airplanes had hit the World Trade Center—one of them an American Airlines jet. Another of our planes hit the Pentagon. United Airlines lost one in New York, and another in a Pennsylvania field when the passengers fought back.

Mom and I watched together as the horror of 9/11 unfolded. Within hours, the government shut down the air space, keeping it like that for almost a week. Every pilot I talked to was in disbelief.

As more details emerged, I learned about the American Airlines jets that had crashed: Flights 11 and 77. I called personnel and some other connections, but no one had any information. Or, if they did, they weren't giving it out. I called other pilots I knew, reaching some or hearing from their families that they had called in and said they were all right. The only one I couldn't find anything out about was Beverley Bass. She was married now and working in American Airlines' 777 school—a prestigious and good-paying position. Beverley had become the first female captain at American Airlines and the second female captain in all the passenger airlines. She'd been on a flight from Paris to New York checking out a pilot, and no one knew what had happened.

Her husband, Tom Stawicki, couldn't find anything out until later in the day when an employee told him her plane was on the ground. The employee didn't know where it was, but this gave him some comfort.

It turned out all incoming European flights had been diverted to Gander, Newfoundland. Newfoundland is an island on the northeast coast of Canada. Its history is rich with aviation, as it was used as a refueling stop during World War II. Many of its streets are named after aviators like Amelia Earhart, Charles Lindbergh, Chuck Yeager, and Eddie Rickenbacker. On 9/11, thirty-eight planes filled with 6,700 passengers and crew landed in a town of 9,400 people. This was a mammoth moment for Gander.

With only 500 hotel rooms, the townsfolk sprang into action to care for the shocked arrivals. First, the passengers learned about the horror of 9/11, suffering a terrible shock the rest of the country had already experienced. Then they discovered the grace of the local people, who opened elementary schools, fire stations, churches, and their homes to care for and feed all 6,700 passengers along with the nineteen animals that had been on board. With the airspace over America shut down for two days, Beverley was stuck in Gander helping organize everything with the other pilots.

Four days after landing, the jets were allowed to leave. Many relationships had been formed. Both the "plane people" and the Gander citizens were forever changed.

It turned out Gander was the only city outside of the United States to house a piece of steel from the Twin Towers. That's how important the town was on 9/11.

Ten years later, Beverley went back to a Gander reunion and found cameras documenting the event. Beverley was the only pilot who returned, and they ended up making a Broadway play—*Come*

From Away—with Beverley as the main character. There is a four-minute, nineteen-second song about her entire aviation life. It may even win a Tony Award.

I rubbed my face, feeling the deep fatigue throughout my body. I wanted to just lie down and go to sleep but was certain I'd feel the cold slap of water when I awoke as the boat capsized. I had to keep going. I was almost there. I could almost smell land.

I glanced down at Duke and noticed the hole in my Crocs was a little bit bigger. This was one smart dog.

"I know I haven't told you much about my brother, Gary, so let's get that out of the way. Are you ready?"

Duke panted happily. He was game for anything, as long as I stayed awake.

Chapter Thirteen

Gary was two years younger than me. He had a lot of Big T in him. Growing up, I didn't spend a lot of time with my brother, especially with Dad working my ass off. We each had our own set of friends, and they rarely mixed.

Gary and I got along just fine. We had a good relationship, but he was always trying to play catch-up with me. After all, I had a two-year head start.

Big T made sure Gary learned to fly. And he found a great teacher—Beverley Bass. She needed the hours, and Gary needed the license. They got to know each other well.

Eventually, Gary stopped playing catch-up and went out to do his own thing. His own thing happened to be partying. He loved the party scene and the group of people that went with it.

Taking after Big T, Gary was a ladies' man. He dated Dallas Cowboys cheerleaders, constantly arriving at parties with drop-dead arm candy. All about the show, he was always ready with a joke—happy-go-lucky, out to have fun. He never had a contentious relationship with anybody, including me.

Because he was a fun-loving guy, he didn't put much emphasis on grades or what it took to accomplish certain goals in life. He was more of an entertainer, the part of Big T that folks adored. When Dad began mentoring him, Gary became more professional.

Everyone liked Gary, so he used that to his advantage. He could get people to do things for him. Unfortunately, he didn't take the time to study the product and learn Dad's designs. Instead, Gary sold the products on his personality and not on his technical knowledge. He scraped by for a long time, because he always had Dad as the backup. If somebody asked a technical question Gary couldn't answer, he'd get Dad to handle it.

In Dad's relationship with his secretary, Marilyn, he was the front man in the aircraft lighting business. But Gary was Dad's *public* front man—the mover, the shaker, the bullshitter. Dad stood behind the scenes with the real information. Believe it or not, a lot of technical products and software are sold that way—with a pretty face in front pouring the drinks, and the smart geek in the background answering the questions.

When Gary was in his late twenties, Big T realized that representing manufacturers of aircraft lighting was a dying field. There were several reasons for this: the major one was money. Big T made more than the president of the company. No president is going to let that happen for long, even if they have to cripple the company with sales. Yet presidents/CEOs aren't stupid. They quickly figured out they could bring some young stud right out of engineering school and do the same thing for a third of the money. But they kept Big T on the team, paying him at his current deal as long as he could produce. This allowed Gary to ride Dad's coattails.

Dad often told me he worried about Gary. He could see that a career in aircraft lighting was becoming a dinosaur, and Gary wasn't preparing himself for the next step. Dad worried that if he died, Gary would be lost. I was pretty sure he was right.

By now, Gary had divorced his first wife. His second marriage was to Kim Bateman, a Dallas Cowboys cheerleader. Her dad, Bob Bateman, was the tower chief at Meacham Field—and I'd known Bob before Gary met Kim. Through Bob, I came to know the FAA bigshots who had an office in the terminal building. Those contacts always came in handy when your chosen field was aviation. Also, it was Bob Bateman who'd answered my call when that line boy dumped the honey bucket all over himself. Bob was the one who'd sent the fire truck to hose the kid down. Like a major airline, life is full of connections.

In our later years, when Gary was working with Dad and I was established with the airlines, Gary and I would meet every day for lunch. Then Dad died in St. Maarten's. Overnight, his meal ticket evaporated.

Gary soon divorced his second wife. Needing a place to live, he bought a house just north of Love Field with a flight attendant he just started dating. His drinking continued.

After several months in the new house, Gary fell sick, throwing up blood all over the place. With his girlfriend traveling all the time, Donna and I had to go and clean it up. It was a complete mess.

With Dad gone and Gary lacking a Plan B, he slowly circled the drain. Floundering around, he left the girl, the house, and Dallas to try his luck in Houston.

Through a high school buddy, he landed a sales job with an oil exploration firm. They needed a guy to wine and dine investors. This meant lots of partying and drinking, the last thing Gary should have been doing. I don't know how well he did, but I suspected Mom was sending him some money every now and then.

During his five years in Houston, he started hanging out with the small-time drug crowd. With no wife and no Big T, Gary took a deeper turn for the worse. I called him out on it, which caused some friction between us.

Mom and I talked him into moving back to Euless and living with her. When he showed up, he was physically in bad shape. Drinking was killing him, ruining his body. Then there was a condition that ran in our family: peptic stomach ulcers. Alcohol is the main enemy of ulcers. My maternal grandfather had died of a ruptured ulcer. Now, Gary was at risk.

Over the next few months, I went to Mom's house early in the morning to find Gary already into the vodka. Mom didn't have the courage or the wherewithal to stop him. Besides, it wasn't her job.

One day, I found Gary with a protruding belly, a sure sign that his liver was failing. When he turned yellow, we put him in the hospital. That's when we started talking—*really* talking.

I learned he'd never recovered from Dad dying. They were very close, working together every day. Big T had been Gary's sun—something he'd orbited around. When that sun exploded, a black hole formed, sucking Gary in. With each drink he took, he went deeper and deeper into the darkness.

The hospital gave Gary a transfusion, stabilizing him. The doctor told us he'd be okay and we could go home. Three hours later, I answered the phone. They wanted us to come right away. Gary had taken a turn for the worse.

When we got there, he was still alive, but it was up to Mom to tell the doctor whether or not to turn off the life support. She made the tough call. I was there at his side on October 14, 2004, when my only brother died. He was fifty.

At the funeral, Beverley Bass showed up. It was great to see her.

Unlike Big T's death, Mom didn't take it well. Gary was her youngest boy. A parent is not supposed to bury a child.

As the funeral ended, we watched his body slip below the earth and disappear. And that was the end of Gary Toler.

Losing a family member is devastating. For the Toler family, we'd been cut in half. Mom and I were the only ones left. Of course, our sadness didn't compare to that of the families who'd lost their loved ones on 9/11. Almost 3,000 people died on that day.

As a result of the terrorist attack, life was different on the plane. The pilots and crew realized that at any moment, any passenger could attack and kill us. I told my crews, "We all need to look out for ourselves. If you see something you don't like, or somebody you don't think we should have on the airplane, jot down the seat number and give it to me. I'll call the company and let them check the person out. They can remove them before we take off, or ground us if we're in the air. Keep your eyes open!"

Soon afterward, the FAA strengthened the cockpit doors, making a lot of changes. Still, it took some time to have all the doors reinforced. We had to be on guard until all the planes were updated.

Another change was security personnel on the plane. Days after 9/11, they ramped up the Air Marshal program. Before 9/11, there'd been a minuscule 33 marshals. In one month, they exploded to 600. Eventually, the ranks climbed to over 4,000. Once they fully implemented these changes, I had at least one air marshal on every flight—and often three. On one flight, I asked this young air marshal, "How much firepower do you have in that backpack?"

"Enough to start a small war," he chuckled. "Or end one."

At first, the air marshal program was not well organized. To board an air marshal, their supervisors would have them come from the operations area down on the ramp level and walk up the jet bridge stairs onto the airplane. Any terrorist with his face up against the glass could spot who it was. All the bad guy had to do was wait until the flight took off and attack that air marshal. With the man neutralized, the terrorist could snatch the marshal's arsenal of weapons and wreak havoc. No need to smuggle your own weapons on board when someone has done the heavy lifting for you.

I complained vigorously about this boarding scheme to management and anyone who'd listen. They finally agreed and went from Plan A to Plan Stupid.

Plan Stupid started at the gate. Before boarding, they made a coded announcement, signaling the air marshals to rise and board first. This saved the terrorist from having to stand up against the glass. Now, he could sit with the rest of the passengers and relax, confident he knew the identity of the air marshal. Once on board, he could take out the air marshal and obtain the small arsenal.

Eventually, they changed that and made the air marshal board with the rest of the passengers. However, they still insisted each air marshal wear a sports jacket, keeping it on during the flight. This was almost as bad as boarding first. It took years to smooth out all the wrinkles.

Right after 9/11, I had a flight from Miami to DFW with a final destination of Phoenix. When I checked in for my flight, I saw a notice that said, "Captain Toler, you will have one passenger named Sweeney who lost a family member on Flight 11 from Boston to L.A. You're to expect numerous Special Services people who are assisting. We appreciate anything you can do to comfort the passenger. Thanks for your help."

As I prepped the plane, I received a second notice that said they'd made a mistake on the passenger's name. "Your traveler will be named William Todd, Madeline Sweeney's father. Madeline Sweeney was a flight attendant on Flight 11. Be advised that gate agents will ask uniformed crew members to board flights before general boarding whenever possible. This procedure will help the captain at checking the identification of all operating crew members and allow the number one flight attendant to review security procedures with all uniformed crew members."

In the flight operations, we had a picture of Madeline Sweeney on the wall. This was just nine days after 9/11.

They brought Madeline's father, William Todd, to first class. He was crying his eyes out. I didn't know what to say, so I looked closely at him, studying his mental state.

I was told he'd already refused to get on two previous flights. He appeared to be too distraught to fly. To help him on this one, Special Services figured that by introducing him to the captain, allowing him to meet me personally, he could get assurances that everything would be fine.

"Well, Mr. Todd," I said, "do you think you're going to be okay to fly?"

When he saw my eyes tearing up, he replied, "I'm okay, Captain. I just want to know if you're okay."

I wiped my eyes. "Yes, sir, everything will be fine."

Before we took off, I had him come up to the cockpit. I showed him my route of flight, the time we were going to get there, and the expected weather along the route. This made him feel comfortable.

I let Mr. Todd sit in the jump seat until it was time for him to go back to first class. He was good during the flight and we made it with no problem.

Fortunately, during my time at American, I never had a security problem on any of my flights. Not once did an air marshal have to deploy. I was thankful not having to deal with a terrorist attack.

In September 2004, I retired from American Airlines after twenty-eight good years. At the time, American was threatening bankruptcy. That was potentially a big problem. They managed half of the pilots' retirement fund. If they went broke, they would keep our money. When they offered a lump sum retirement package, I took it.

Ever since my divorce, I had been heading up to Lake Texoma and spending time on the boat. There, I met Julie and began dating her for several years. Unfortunately, I kept hearing she kept company with other men. That soured the relationship, but for some reason—mostly loneliness—I kept seeing her. We even traveled together overseas.

Needing something to do after flying commercial jets for a living, I followed in Big T's footsteps and worked on my sea captain skills. In late 2005, I earned my Master of Steam or Motor Vessels USCG License. This took a lot of work, including learning celestial navigation. With this license, I could handle larger boats like yachts.

With the classroom part of the license completed, I worked on the required sea time as a crew member on larger vessels. Finally, on March 23, 2006, I was awarded the endorsement to my license: Master of Steam or Motor Vessels of not more than 100 Gross Registered Tons (Domestic Tonnage) Upon or Near Coastal Waters. For some reason, the Coast Guard failed to administer my oath while I was in Houston. At their expense, they flew the officer-in-charge, S. Mingus, USCG, up to Dallas to swear me in as a USCG Merchant Marine 100 Ton Master Captain. It was a strange event, but now I was official.

To fill my long days, I hired out as a delivery boy to captain yachts to rich people. Before my license, I had been bringing yachts to Texas from Florida. On my first one, I rode with a good friend, Harold Mitchell. We brought his 42-foot Bertram to Lake Texoma. Then I brought my second boat, a 43-foot Hatteras motor yacht, to the same lake. Later, I helped another great friend, Bill Reeves, bring his 58-foot Bertram from Toronto, Canada, through the Great Lakes to Chicago. That was fun.

The longest run I made was for a customer of Jan and Mike Joyce. The Joyces owned Hargrave Custom Yachts in Ft. Lauderdale, which builds yachts from 100 to 136 feet long. Their primary business, though, is in the 100-foot category.

The Joyces called me with a problem. They had a customer in New York who wanted them to build him a yacht, but he needed to sell his current boat—a 68-foot SonShip. I flew to New York and started on the journey to Ft. Lauderdale with the owner, who insisted on coming along.

The owner was a nice man, but the trip was challenging. Even though I was the captain, he ran the boat outside the USCG rules of the road whenever he was at the helm. We were pulled over three separate times by game wardens because he ran too fast in manatee zones. On one occasion, he stormed into the harbor so fast that he wiped out the porcelain china on a yacht docked in the harbor. I'm surprised we didn't get thrown in jail. But he handed over the credit card and new china was purchased instantly.

This trip was supposed to be eleven days, but it took a month due to Hurricane Wilma. The big storm had ripped through Ft. Lauderdale, knocking out the electricity for two weeks. We had to wait for the area to open up. Then we were met with hundreds of other boats heading there, clogging up the Intracoastal Waterway. It was a disaster.

To move large boats like that, it really takes three people. You're operating them 24/7. You need two people at the helm: one person navigating and looking out for the channel/day markers, and another person driving the boat. The third person should be getting rest. However, you can do it on the cheap with two. It's just draining, and you have to pull over to get some sleep. Pulling over a yacht or setting the anchor is not always a guaranteed proposition.

I did ten yacht deliveries during my delivery career, earning $100 a day. The pay was terrible, but I loved the experience. It reminded me of my earlier days in a plane, trying to build up my logbook hours.

During my time on the water, I learned about the Great Loop. The Great Loop is a large circle running through the Great Lakes to Chicago, down through the Illinois River to the Mississippi River, on to New Orleans and out to the Gulf of Mexico. The rest of the loop skirts the coastline all the way around Florida and up the East Coast to Chesapeake Bay, then through the Elk River to the Delaware River, around Pennsylvania to New York, up the Hudson River to the Mohawk River, and back to the Great Lakes. The entire loop is 6,000 miles long! It's like driving from the East Coast to the West Coast and back, and then another 600 miles. Completing the Great Loop in one continuous trip takes over two months. Others do it in pieces, while most captains like me have never completed it.

There's a group that supports people making this journey—America's Great Loop Cruisers' Association. Members along the loop will let you dock your boat and stay with them, sometimes for no charge. Of course, they check you out to make sure you're truly a Great Looper.

The association has a chat room to find places to dock, good restaurants, and where to get fuel. It's a necessity to join that organization when navigating the Great Loop. And you meet great people.

My original boat needed a name. Thinking about my lovely wife, I christened it the *Prima D*. When I upgraded to a bigger boat, I wanted to keep the name. That meant undergoing a formal christening ceremony.

Like baptizing a person, there is a big ceremony for launching a new boat. In this case, we were christening a new name to a used boat. I paid for a retired Navy corpsman to do the honors. He was like a preacher, reading the official Navy prayer. The idea was to ask God to protect those in the boat and make sure it always made it to land. Also, sailors are very superstitious. They constantly worry about bad luck. Christening a boat is supposed to bring good luck.

I had friends out to the dock for the big ceremony. We had drinks and snacks to celebrate the christening. When the ceremony was over, I was told to get on board so I could be saluted as the captain. Now the boat was ready for service. I hoped it would never let me down.

As I said earlier, the partying at Lake Texoma got old—literally. The kids were younger, and the crowd changed every five years. Through it all, I remained. I thought about selling my boat. Then something amazing happened. A dog entered my life and changed my future. How I got him is a big story. Now it's time to tell it.

Chapter Fourteen

Dogs have always been in my life. From as far back as I can remember, we had a dog. One of them was a dachshund named Fritzie. He was a great dog, barking and letting us know if anything was amiss in the Toler household.

As I grew older, Mom bought some poodles—Bingo and Brandy. They were smart dogs. And boy, did they love their mother! Then I met Donna, a true dog lover.

Donna had Corgis growing up in Detroit. She couldn't have any when she worked for American Airlines. It wasn't that American told her they were forbidden. It just wasn't practical to be gone three days straight with a pet at home. It wasn't fair to the dog.

When we married and Donna quit American Airlines, she talked me into buying a Corgi. I said, "If you can find one, I'll get it for you." A minute later, she started looking.

Later that week, I was playing golf when Donna called the golf pro in the pro shop. "What hole is Toler on?" she asked him.

"Gosh, I don't know," the pro replied. "Is it an emergency?"

"No, it's not an emergency. But if you see him, tell him he needs to come home because we need to go get a Corgi."

The pro gave me the message and I made a beeline home—like a good dog.

We drove to a breeder in Dallas and purchased a male. We—or Donna—named him Jamie. He lived sixteen good years.

When Jamie was five, we went back to the same breeder and bought a female we named Casey. She lasted fifteen years.

As Jamie and Casey grew older, Donna dragged me to the Fort Worth Coliseum for a dog show. There we met a vet, Dr. Sharon Wild, who was showing some Corgis. She had one-year-old Dooley. We both fell in love with this little guy. Dr. Wild let us play with Dooley for a bit. We left our names, hoping she'd part with the young Corgi.

Back home, Donna spent the next month burning up the phone lines to Dr. Wild, begging her to sell Dooley. She refused.

Then one day, Dr. Wild called and said she'd consider letting us adopt Dooley. But he was a show dog. We would have to agree to show him.

A few days later, she came to the house and administered a full-fledged interview. She wanted to see how we were going to treat Dooley, where he would stay, and what kind of life he would have with us. Needless to say, she was very cautious.

As she examined every nook and cranny of our house, she spotted our two Corgis. When she checked them out and saw how well they were cared for, we won the Dooley sweepstakes. All we had to do now was show the dog—whatever that entailed.

It turns out showing a dog is hard work. Donna did most of it, traveling on a show circuit long enough to discover it wasn't a fun way to live. During this time, Donna became good friends with Dr. Wild. She showed Dooley three times before getting permission from the doctor to stop. That was the end of our dog show career.

Dooley was eight when Donna and I divorced. She got custody of him.

Living by herself, Donna went out and bought another Corgi— Mickey. For a few years, she went on a Corgi buying spree, finding Dylan and Darby. Donna is Corgi crazy.

During my time with Donna, I learned so much about dogs, their needs, their signals, and their behavior. Little did I know, she was setting me up to have the best dog in the whole world.

It all started one cold and rainy morning. I was sitting at my kitchen table having breakfast, staring out at the gray sky. Julie lived separately in a townhome she rented. I had been trying to break up with Julie for ten years but couldn't make it stick. It was hard being lonely all the time.

I had just taken a sip of coffee when the phone rang. It was Julie. "Tom, I've got something I want you to see."

"What is it?" I asked, certain it was way too early for playing games.

"I'm not going to tell you. You just have to come over and see it."

With nothing better to do, I drove to her townhome and found her with Carlos, a friend of hers. I had met Carlos before. He drove a wrecker and repossessed cars.

I went inside to escape the rain and sat on her couch, with Julie on a loveseat to my left and Carlos sitting directly across from me in an overstuffed recliner—the man-of-the-house chair, the one I used to occupy. As Carlos bored a hole through me, a brief thought went through my brain. *Why the hell am I here?*

Julie told Carlos to tell me his story. I leaned back and rolled my eyes, waiting to see how a repo man sleeping with my soon-to-be ex-girlfriend could possibly surprise me.

At two in the morning, Carlos said he'd been hooking up a car at an apartment complex. Worried that someone was coming, he ducked behind a dumpster to see if his cover was blown. As he kicked at the nasty trash spilling out of the dumpster, he heard a yelp. Down at his feet was a puppy, foraging for food. Apparently, the little guy had been left outside in the cold and rain to fend for himself. With the dumpster overflowing, he had kind of made it his home.

Carlos picked up the puppy and put him in his warm cab. When his shift was over, he transferred the dog to his car and drove to Julie's house. Now she was trying to figure out a way to keep the dog, even though her rental rules prevented it.

Before I arrived, Julie had called her daughter to see if she wanted the dog. The daughter did but had the same rental-rule problems as

Julie. That's where things stood when I walked into her utility room and spotted a five-week-old puppy in the corner shaking like a leaf.

I bent down, inspected him, and shook my head. "Man, I don't know about this," I said. "Let me think about it."

I left the scared puppy at Julie's place and called my ex-wife and now good friend Donna. She always had great advice when it came to dogs.

We met for lunch a few hours later at TGI Friday's and I told her the story. "What do you think about me having a dog?" I asked her.

"Go for it, Tom!" she said.

Unconvinced, I kept asking her questions about food, vets, and anything else I could think of to delay my decision. All she kept saying was, "Just go get the dog. You need something like that in your life."

I sighed and drove back to Julie's townhome. "How about I take the dog?" I said.

"I don't know, Tom," she replied. "I'm getting attached to him."

"Listen," I told her, completely unaware that she was about to make a life-or-death decision affecting both me and the dog, "you'd better make sure you're going to keep him, because this is the only offer I'm going to make."

She hesitated, looked back at the dog, and bit her lip. A minute later, she picked up the puppy and handed him to me. I was now a dog owner.

I drove home and conducted a more detailed inspection of my new house guest. He was obviously underfed. And he was constantly licking his tail. I checked it out.

Embedded in the skin were parts of a rubber band—a poor man's attempt at docking it. This meant the owners may have wanted to show him. For some reason, they'd let him escape or dumped him off without removing the rubber band. This created a painful throbbing for the poor dog. He had been gnawing at his tail for days, hoping to end the pain. Somehow, he'd snagged enough of it to release the rubber band, leaving behind some evidence for me to find. I carefully removed the extra bits and soon he felt better.

That afternoon, I took him to a vet for a checkup. She was fairly certain he was an Australian Cattle Dog, also nicknamed a Red Heeler or Blue Heeler. She explained that this breed averages forty to forty-five pounds and is used for herding cattle and horses. They have a little dingo in them, so they're agile and wily. She cautioned me that he needed lots of exercise. I figured that would be good for me too.

"What do you want to call him?" the vet asked.

"Duke," I said. "His name is Duke."

"That's nice. How did you come up with that?"

I explained how Jimmy Stewart had told me that John Wayne had had a dog named Duke when he was growing up. His family started calling him Duke, and the nickname stuck throughout his career. Now it would be my dog's name. If it was good enough for John Wayne, it was good enough for me.

The vet measured Duke's teeth and figured he was close to six weeks old. We set his birthday at March 14, 2007. I had the vet give him all the proper shots. As she was finishing up, she noticed he was underfed. "Dogs aren't usually weaned off until seven or eight weeks. Since you don't have access to the mother, just feed him puppy food. He should start putting on weight."

This vet was expensive, but Duke left her with a clean bill of health and an approximate date to get him fixed. I was sure he wouldn't be looking forward to that.

Duke and I bonded instantly. Since my home backed up to a golf course, he spent a lot early morning time running around on the fairway. Sometimes I'd take him in the golf cart with me. We went everywhere together.

In no time, he'd met all my friends, becoming a topic of conversation. He also adored me, which is a great way to get on my good side.

About a month after I had taken Duke into my home, I was driving him back from seeing Donna and opened the car door thinking he'd jump out and head to the front door. Instead, he took off running through the neighborhood. Believe me, Australian Cattle Dogs can fly.

I watched in horror as a Mercedes sideswiped him, its brakes screeching. I ran to the stopped car, but it took off before I could talk to the driver. Looking down, I saw Duke's dark blood splattered on the pavement, but no Duke. That's when I broke the glass on my imaginary life emergency button and called the only person I knew who could help me: Donna.

Once she assured me she was on the way, I called the police. The local officer said he'd keep an eye out.

When Donna arrived, she took responsibility for searching the golf course. As she disappeared between the houses, I climbed back in my car and drove through the neighborhood. I twisted my head this way and that, hoping to find a trace of my dog.

It just so happened the policeman I called was also the animal control officer. With one call, he had the police looking everywhere. After five hard hours of searching, the police, Donna, and I had struck out. It was time for me to face the fact that Duke was gone and there was no getting him back.

As I drove up to my house, I saw him sitting in the driveway, waiting for his master. I jumped out of the car intensely angry but overjoyed to see my buddy. He knew where he belonged. I guess he'd just wanted to stretch his legs and check out the neighborhood. You know, leave some peemail around for his new neighbors to check out.

I looked over Duke and found he hadn't been injured by the car. The "blood" I thought I'd seen turned out to be diarrhea. Who wouldn't have that if they got hit by a car?

By late August, Duke had been with me for four months. He was six months old and not putting on any weight. Instead of going back to the original vet, I took him to several local vets who were lower priced. They examined him and ran tests. After seeing five different doctors, none of them could figure anything out.

The last one I saw wanted to keep Duke and try different treatments on him. After I left Duke with him for a week, a friend told me about a world-class veterinarian program at College Station, home of the Texas A&M Aggies. In fact, the College of Veterinary Medicine was legendary. Not only did it train a majority of the state's veterinarians, but it was ranked in the top five of all veterinary schools in the country. I went to the vet's office in Fort Worth and picked up Duke. (It turned out later this vet was indicted for keeping dogs until they died and harvesting their organs for transplants to other dogs— basically an organ harvesting factory for rich dog owners willing to pay big bucks to keep Fifi alive.)

I drove Duke down to College Station and found this legendary vet school. Of course, the average person doesn't just show up with a sick dog. I needed a referral from another vet, someone with connections. Fortunately, connections were part of my toolkit.

I handed Duke over to a vet who said they would call me at the hotel I was staying at and let me know when they had something. For the next two days, I explored the world of Aggies, learning way more than I cared to about their lives and culture. It was like living among a tribe of Native Americans—or in a cult.

On the third day, I was very close to painting my face Aggie maroon and donating all my money to the university when I realized I hadn't heard from the vet school. Since my first year of college had been spent at the University of Texas in Austin—bitter rivals of Aggies—and my DNA was burnt orange, I decided I had to get out of town before I jumped over to the dark side. Packing my bags, I was just about to close the hotel door when the phone rang.

"You can come and get Duke," the clerk told me.

I drove over and paid the whopping $1,100 bill. "What's wrong with him?" I asked the vet.

"We can't figure it out," he said.

I was stunned. "Is he going to die?"

"We don't know. We just don't know."

"Thanks for nothing," I mumbled as Duke and I reunited. I loaded him in the car. After enjoying ten minutes of face licking, we headed north for home.

It was a sad drive, with tears running down my face. By now, my relationship with Julie was over. My marriage was gone. My mother was suffering through lung cancer, a result of smoking all her life. In and out of the hospital, her days were numbered.

I kept looking at Duke as if he was going to disappear. In all my life, I'd never really opened my heart to anyone, always keeping my relationships at a safe distance. After seeing Mom hurt by Dad's relationship with Marilyn, I didn't want that to happen to me. I'd also allowed my career ambitions to cloud my judgment and interfere with my personal relationships. Other than having Duke next to me, I felt so alone. Now I was going to lose him. It was all so sad.

Duke tried to cheer me up, sitting in my lap and lovingly gazing at me. This made it hard to steer, but I didn't care. I wanted to soak up every second of love I could.

I arrived home and sat at my kitchen table crying. I stopped for an hour to eat dinner, then cried all night. Somewhere near midnight, I had a thought. *You know, I never gave that first vet a shot. She's expensive, but I don't care about that now. I wonder what she can do.*

I took Duke back to see her and explained everything I'd been through. She wanted me to leave him there for a few days and see what she could find. I had nothing to lose. Duke was probably going to die, and she might as well take a shot.

A few days later, I answered her call. "Tom, come up here. I need to talk to you."

I arrived in the lobby and waited for them to escort me to an examination room. I noticed Duke wasn't there.

I nervously waited, staring at the stipple on the walls. When the doctor entered the room, I tried to discern what I was about to hear. She closed the door and slapped a file on the table.

"Well, Tom, I've got some good news—maybe it's good news—but mostly bad news."

My chest sank. "What's the good news?"

"We discovered what's wrong with him. He has dysautonomia. It's an autoimmune nerve deficiency within the digestive system. Basically, the dog starves to death because he can't hold food down. There's not much written about it because it's very rare. It was discovered in Missouri, mostly among cattle and horses."

"Oh," was all I could say, tears welling up in my eyes.

"Look, let me try a regimen of drugs, medicines, and whatever I can to see if we can at least get him to the point where he can start digesting some of his food. I'm going to start with Reglan and see how that does. But I need you to check his poop, see if it's solid. That's what we're shooting for. I need you to keep a good log of each poop. Can you do that?"

"Doctor, keeping logs is something I know a thing or two about."

I gave her my credit card, not caring how much was charged. This dog and I were now best friends. I needed to do anything possible to keep him alive.

I went home and called Donna, giving her the diagnosis. As word got around, I received call after call from friends checking on Duke's poop. It turned into a daily Poop Report, much like weather and stocks. They never wanted to talk to me much—just find out if he was holding down food and the consistency of his latest bowel movement.

Between meals and pooping, I walked Duke around the neighborhood, spending a lot of time with him. I knew our days were numbered and wanted to squeeze every bit of life out of him. This bonded us even more—if that was possible.

With careful experimentation and lots of hard work, we finally stumbled on a combination of medicine and food Duke could handle. The magic food I found was Freshpet. It's kept in the refrigerated section. It lacks preservatives so it's perishable. Sure enough, one year later, Duke had filled out into a full-grown dog. It was a beautiful thing to see.

Early on in our relationship, I found Duke to be very protective. The first person he allowed into his circle of trust was Donna. He seemed to accept her as his momma. When I traveled out of town, Donna took care of him at her house. She was very good to him. As Duke met more of her friends, he turned into a friendly, loving dog.

One aspect of raising Duke was his energy level. With food sticking to his ribs, he was ready to run all the time. I couldn't always give him the workout he needed. Searching the neighborhood, I found someone who came to the house and walked/ran him every day. This suited him just fine.

Fourteen months into my new life as a dog owner, I experienced a major hurt in another part of my life. Mom was near the end. She'd been in and out of Baylor Hospital. Donna had visited her every day. They were extremely close—best friends, as they described each other. When we had to transfer Mom to the hospice, she lasted one day. At eighty-one, my mother, Robbie Helen Toler, was gone.

Donna and I were crushed. All I could see lying there in the bed was my laughing and fun-loving mother. She was never serious or dour. She was the parent who said, "Hey, I love you." She was the one to give us a hug. It was Mom who kissed us when we were scared or hurting. She made it all better. And it was Mom who said the critical words any kid needs to hear, "I'm proud of you. You did good."

Mom's funeral was upbeat, not somber—just the way she would've wanted it. It was crowded. Even Dad's coworkers from Grimes in Urbana, Ohio, attended.

When the last shovel of dirt was dropped on her casket, it was just Duke and me. The oldest son of the Toler family, with no children or spouse, was all alone.

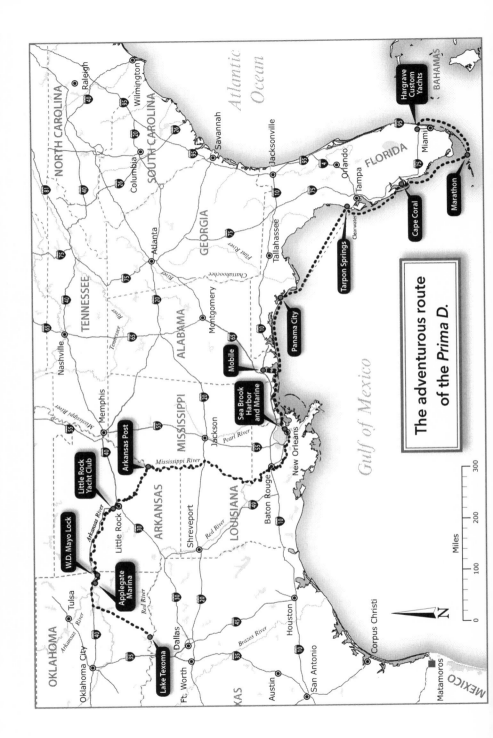

The adventurous route of the *Prima D.*

Chapter Fifteen

With my best buddy Duke getting stronger by the day, I turned my attention to the *Prima D*. A buddy of mine told me he had a close friend at the Corps of Engineers. One of the Corps' responsibilities involved monitoring the water levels at Lake Texoma. He said this engineer had some dramatic news, and urged me to call him.

When I reached the engineer, he said, "If you don't get your boat out of there in the next two weeks, it might be there for at least two years. The lake is drying up so fast, the travel lift won't be able to pull your boat out."

I pondered his advice. For the past few months, each time I'd driven to Grand Pappy Point Marina, I'd seen the levels dropping. If I left my boat there, eventually I'd have to walk down a steep embankment and out over the dried lakebed. Hauling supplies to and from the boat would be exhausting. With six months to go before I turned sixty, this wasn't something I wanted to do.

As I said before, I was getting too old for the party crowd. It just wasn't fun anymore. With Julie out of the picture and no prospects in sight, trips to the lake weren't a priority. As painful as it was, my only option was to sell the *Prima D*.

Selling a large yacht on a freshwater lake is tough. Any interested boater knows that hauling it to the Gulf is a very expensive proposition. It's like selling the largest home on the street. The per square foot price is reduced. Add in the falling lake levels, and a buyer would have to do the same thing as I would—toting his supplies for hundreds of yards. And forget the fact they'd be boating on a smaller lake footprint, crowding all the watercraft together. How much fun could you have in that scenario? There was no way around it. Selling to a local would mean taking a severe price reduction.

The more I thought about it, the more that didn't seem right. The *Prima D* had taken good care of me. She had a heart and a soul. I wanted her to be taken care of. If I sold to some local boater at a reduced price, he might not take care of her. She could turn ugly and rot in no time. That would distress me. No, I couldn't sell to a local, even if I was willing to take less money. I'd have to consider Plan B.

I picked up the phone and called a buddy of mine, Harold Mitchell. I'd known Harold for over twenty years, starting when Donna bought me my first boat. It had happened to be in the stall next to Harold's boat. Harold and I had ended up spending time together on the lake, and even took a few boat trips together. I trusted Harold and knew he'd give me good advice.

We discussed Plan B: removing the *Prima D* from the lake and sailing it to Ft. Lauderdale. I contacted the agent I'd bought it from, Mike Joyce. He was still in business. He agreed to find a buyer for me if I could bring it to Ft. Lauderdale. To do that, there were only two options. The first was hauling the boat south to Houston or Freeport and floating her in the Gulf of Mexico. This would be very expensive, but at least I'd be that much closer to the east coast of Florida. Starting in the Gulf was the fastest way to get there.

The other option was to have the boat hauled north and hook up with the Arkansas River in Oklahoma. The Arkansas River could get me to the Mississippi River, which let out into the Gulf. It was a much longer journey by boat, but the transport was cheaper.

As I weighed the options, I considered the adventure aspect of this trip. I'd be leaving Duke in Donna's capable hands, so he would be fine. And Harold had agreed to be my first mate if I went the Arkansas River route.

I studied the map and waterways. If we went north, Harold and I would have to be on top of our game. We'd have to carefully navigate through locks and under low bridges. We'd have to spot navigational buoys and pick up local information on the dredged channels to stay in. Then there was the mighty Mississippi. We'd have to watch out for heavily loaded barges and other traffic. I had to choose between an adventure and a longer journey, or a quicker trip with higher transport costs. Since this was my last hurrah, and it would be considerably cheaper, I chose the northern route. Oklahoma and the Arkansas River it was.

Sitting at my desk, I stared at a photo of me celebrating my hole in one. I'd been so young then. Now, my fifties were almost burned-out embers. I hated to sell something that had been such a part of me for so long, but it was time. At least I'd get one last adventure out of it.

It was midnight when I took Duke out to take care of his business. Once he was done, we retired to my bedroom. I climbed under the sheets and heard him sorting out his place at the foot of my bed. With the lights out, I recalled so many great memories on Lake Texoma. There was Donna and me for years, bringing Corgis on board. Then she was gone and it was me and Julie. This was followed by me and nobody else. Memory after memory flooded my mind. Eventually, I drifted off to sleep.

I arrived at the Grand Pappy Point Marina in Lake Texoma to see my boat waiting for me. It was a melancholy feeling, walking onto the *Prima D* for the last time in this lake. Selling this boat meant cutting all ties to my youth. In six months, I'd turn sixty. By then, the *Prima D* would be in Ft. Lauderdale and I would be a permanent landlubber. It felt like an era was dying. And it was. I was leaving the land of middle-aged and heading toward elderly. But I still had one last great adventure to take. I planned on soaking up every bit of it I could.

The travel lift had been shifted into place, ready for the moving crew to do their thing. When they arrived, they climbed on board and took down the flybridge, stowing it on the bow. This was a time-consuming and delicate process. All electrical, hydraulic, and mechanical connections had to be severed. Once this was done, the yacht was lifted from the lake, water dripping off the sides like tears.

The travel lift rolled forward away from the lake, carrying the boat like a baby. Straddling the long trailer, the men lowered it in place, tapping in hull supports to ensure the *Prima D* didn't move or shift during the trip. With that done, they took a break and waited for midnight, when we'd sneak across the border and head for the Robert Kerr Reservoir.

In preparing for our trip, we had constructed a tight schedule. We needed to make a certain amount of progress each day. Yet by the time the *Prima D* arrived in Sallisaw and was reassembled, we were a full day behind. This was a bad start.

The sky was black as we dressed and made our way to the boat. A café at the Applegate Marina put a hearty breakfast in our bellies. With that behind us, at seven a.m. we climbed on board the *Prima D* and set off thirty minutes later on my last great adventure.

Our first challenge was a lock. Our radio wasn't completely working when we made it through the forty-four-foot drop. An hour later, we dropped another twenty-two feet at the W.D. Mayo lock. Passing a few towboats and barges, we managed to make three-plus hours on the river before running into our first challenge: the engines were shutting down.

Harold helped me anchor under a bridge so we could check it out.

"What do you think it is?" he asked me.

"I don't know, but I hope we didn't take on some bad fuel."

The *Prima D* ran on diesel. To sort out the impurities in the fuel, the two engines were equipped with tall Racor filters. As Harold and I crawled down there and checked them out, we found the viewing glass cloudy when it should've been a clear orange. This meant we had water in the fuel.

We changed the filters, but could only get the engines running for a brief time. An expert we called gave us a procedure that got the port engine running, but not the starboard. We switched to a smaller tank in the bow and changed the filters again, managing to make some headway.

With the constant fuel problems, we fell way behind. After three days on the river, we limped into the Little Rock Yacht Club. I docked the boat and called for a mechanic to clean out the fuel tanks. It was the only way to get the *Prima D* running again.

Unfortunately, it wasn't long before I received a call from the marina. They had spotted us leaking diesel fuel. With the engines not running properly, the *Prima D* sent out the uncombusted and waterlogged fuel. The slick around the dock was nasty. As soon as I saw it, I knew it was trouble.

Any boat that leaks diesel fuel can be impounded and/or fined for the massive cleanup needed to clear the lake of diesel fuel. We're talking tens of thousands, if not hundreds of thousands, of dollars. I absolutely did not want to deal with that.

Early the next morning, Harold walked the entire row of boat-houses with a special bottle. By spraying dishwashing liquid mixed with water over the oil, the oil dispersed into tiny clusters before sinking to the bottom of the lake. It's not good for the environment, but it gets rid of the visible oil slick.

No sooner had we solved that problem than I discovered that nothing in the wheelhouse worked. The transport crew had failed to hook up the electronics properly. Fortunately, we didn't need it to navigate down the Arkansas River, but we would on the Mississippi River and in the Gulf.

I discussed all this with Harold, and he decided to go back home while I procured a mechanic to fix everything. Depending on how long the repairs would take, I might go home too. As Harold packed up, the marina told us to get out. No doubt they had seen our attempt to kill the oil slick and wanted us gone. I shook my head in disgust. This adventure was quickly turning into a nightmare.

Three weeks passed before I returned to Little Rock. From what I could tell, the fuel tanks had been repaired. I was on board getting things ready when Harold arrived. He brought with him Bill Reeves, another friend of mine. The three of us would get the *Prima D* to the Gulf.

Before we could cast off, the refrigerator stopped working. I called a local repairman and spent more money fixing that. Man, this money-saving trip was beginning to cost me.

Finally, we loaded up on provisions and got underway.

It wasn't long before we noticed a light slick trailing behind us. That meant we still had some combustion problems. I needed to get to New Orleans where I could have it fixed. More delays and more money.

Trailing diesel also translated into terrible gas mileage. With good conditions, we should've been able to make 250 miles on the tanks we had on board. We also had another fifty-gallon drum in reserve. With the way things were going, I needed to fill up each day. This was not always possible.

Diesel fuel is used by the bigger boats. On the smaller rivers, with fewer yachts, the demand for diesel is lower. Thus, there are fewer suppliers. I would have to get creative and tap into some local knowledge to get the fuel we needed.

By the end of the first day, we arrived at a rundown marina just past Pine Bluff, Arkansas, only to discover they didn't carry diesel. I was seriously beginning to question the sanity of this trip.

Somehow, we made it to the Mississippi River. Running very low on fuel, we had no choice but to turn upstream. A refueling station was ten miles away. It was our only choice.

If I thought finding fuel on the smaller Arkansas River was tough, the Mississippi was downright mean. The fuel suppliers only wanted to pump 4,000 to 5,000 gallons for tugboats, not 250 gallons for private yachts. And the nozzles didn't fit. But with a thick wad of cash, I was able to finagle some fuel.

Fueled up, we turned around and headed south, pushing hard down the mighty river. This involved dodging tugboats and barges. Trust me, we needed all three sets of eyes looking out for trouble. One mistake and we'd all go under, because the mighty Mississippi is no place for wimps.

Chapter Sixteen

"What's the word?" Harold asked me.

"The word is Panama City. The part we need to fix the generator is there."

"Damn!" Bill said, wiping the sweat from his face. "That's a long way to go."

"Maybe it'll get cooler the closer we get to the coast."

"Yeah, and maybe I'll win the lottery," Harold muttered.

I knew they were hot, and it wasn't just the temperature. The cabin was unbearable, despite every porthole and window fully opened. We had lost the generator, and that meant the air conditioner was out. The electronics and water pump were gone too. If I didn't know any better, I would think the *Prima D* didn't want to get to Ft. Lauderdale.

Still leaking fuel, we pushed hard for New Orleans. I had called ahead and talked to the manager of the Seabrook Harbor and Marine. It was on the industrial canal between the river and Lake Pontchartrain. Seabrook would be a great spot to tie up and leave the boat. I knew with the problems we had, I'd have to get the *Prima D* repaired before moving on.

We arrived at the canal only to find the lock blocked to us. Too much traffic was coming out of Lake Pontchartrain for us to get in. By the time we were cleared, we had missed curfew. Now the bridges were locked down to accommodate rush hour automobile traffic.

With no choice, we anchored outside the lock for almost two hours until the bridge opened and let us continue to the marina. We arrived near seven—hot, tired, irritated, and out of beer.

I told Bill and Harold we were shutting it down and leaving the boat here. They didn't object.

For the next few hours, we sealed up the boat and locked it down. We spent the night in a motel before renting a car and driving back to Texas. All three of us had had enough fun on the Mississippi. I looked forward to getting home, sliding into my own bed, and seeing my best buddy Duke.

It was New Year's Day 2012. Duke and I celebrated by going on a long walk. Usually, my neighborhood helper did this, but I figured Duke and I had been apart for so long that we needed to spend time together. Plus, I wanted some fresh air, and Duke needed the exercise.

Over the next week, I spent a lot of time with Duke. We walked and played, growing even closer. I couldn't imagine life without him.

At the end of the new year's first week, I said goodbye to Duke and drove with Harold to the Big Easy. We found the *Prima D* just as we'd left it.

I had arranged for a mechanic to meet me there, and he arrived on time. I wanted these problems solved before we headed out.

The mechanic discovered the fuel cooler—the device that let in fresh water to cool the engines—was cracked and letting fuel out into the return water. That's why we'd been laying a slick. And we had an antifreeze leak along with a leaking water pump. This forced us to wait several days for parts to come in. During this time, we took care of some minor maintenance issues, including a leaking lavatory in the forward head.

Eventually, the parts arrived and we were able to cast off from New Orleans. However, we'd burned through eight days and a lot of cash to fix the boat. It seemed like my bank account had also sprung a leak, trailing cash from Oklahoma all the way down the Mississippi. Yet I felt confident the problems were all behind us as I guided the *Prima D* down the Intracoastal and on our way to Florida. This trip had to get better.

Begging for fuel here and there on the Intracoastal, we arrived in Mobile, Alabama, at around five in the afternoon, hungry and tired. Still, it'd been a great day. We were making progress. Things were looking up.

Then they weren't.

At the marina, I started feeling sick. Something was wrong. I knew my body.

Harold and I discussed the new development and decided I needed to get back to Dallas to see a doctor. The next morning, I drafted a laundry list of items I wanted done to the boat and left it at the marina. After he charged my card $30,000, the owner assured me he'd take good care of the *Prima D* and put her back in tiptop shape. He loaded us in his truck and drove us back to New Orleans. Harold and I transferred everything to my truck and drove straight back to Dallas.

As soon as I hit Dallas, I went to see my doctor. He ran some tests and didn't like what he saw. Recently, I'd been to Costa Rica. I'd spent a lot of time deep sea fishing, catching my share of yellowfin tuna. Each night, the locals had grilled the freshly caught tuna over open pits and served it up. I'd eaten a ton of fish on that trip.

My doctor informed me I had high levels of mercury in my blood. At room temperature, mercury is a liquid. It migrates to the joints and the brain. Add in a life of drinking and partying, and my liver was struggling to rid my body of the mercury. The doctor said bluntly, "We measure mercury poisoning on a scale of one to ten. You're an eighteen!"

That got my attention.

He put me on a regimen designed to improve my liver and flush out the mercury. Still, he gave me no guarantees I'd make it.

A few months after my initial diagnosis, the marina in Mobile called and wanted to charge another $20,000 on my card. I was too sick to refuse or investigate further. I gave them permission.

Working hard, I spent the next year struggling to recover. I could do nothing but follow the doctor's orders and wait. Sometimes it felt like I was waiting for my own death.

Slowly but surely, I started getting back on my feet. When it looked like the worst was past, I had some friends over to celebrate my recovery. During the party, I walked upstairs to grab something and tripped coming back down. Apparently, I hit the marble tile hard, cutting my head open and busting my shoulder. I didn't know for sure what happened because I was knocked out.

At this point, this page should have information about my funeral—excerpts from the eulogies by my friends, and pictures to remember me by. That should be the end of the book. But it isn't. I had an ace up my sleeve. That ace was Duke.

With his sensitive hearing, he picked up the thud through the loud music and conversation. Trotting over to the stairs, he found me, bleeding and unconscious.

Dogs are smarter than we give them credit for, because this special Blue Heeler started yelling like the house was on fire. His barking drew the attention of one of my friends. He came and found me before immediately calling an ambulance.

It wasn't long before I headed to surgery. The doctors sewed up my head and operated on my shoulder. (Later, I'd need a second shoulder operation to fully repair it.)

As soon as I arrived home from the hospital, I showered Duke with love. No telling how long I would have lain there unconscious and bleeding before eventually dying. Duke had saved my life.

It took me another three long months to recover. The physical therapy was brutal. When the doctor said I could travel, I was overjoyed.

One bright and clear summer day, I loaded up Duke and drove to Mobile, Alabama. I wanted to surprise the marina and see what $50,000 had bought me.

I arrived on a Sunday and slipped past the office. Duke and I looked everywhere, but couldn't find the *Prima D*. We shuffled down a path leading to a bayou deep in the swamp before finally spotting her. I was stunned.

My boat was tied off to a rickety post. All around it were sawgrass and old tree limbs sticking out of stagnant water. The hull looked terrible, like it hadn't been touched in years.

Before stepping on my boat, I noticed snakes crawling out of the water, slithering up the broken trees. Like the owner of the marina, they smelled a fresh sucker.

If I thought I was mad at seeing all this, I was in for an even bigger surprise. As I placed my foot over the threshold, I felt some fabric through my tennis shoe. Once I was fully on the boat, I spotted my father's American flag—the one that had been draped over his coffin. These losers had placed the flag on the deck, using it as a doormat. My blood boiled.

I picked up the flag, hanging it from some hooks. It was completely ruined.

I made my way around the cabin and found all the rugs pulled up. Every piece of furniture had been turned upside down. As hard as it was to believe, the interior was worse than the exterior.

I stood there raging for a while. Duke stared at me, making sure I wouldn't have a heart attack. Once I calmed down, my brain started working. It was time to get even.

I pulled out my camera and adjusted the lens. Slowly and with a determined purpose, I snapped off forty-six photos to use as evidence later. Then I walked to the office and blew a gasket.

The clerk manning the desk was incapable of dealing with me or the situation. I could tell he had no idea how my boat had been treated. He called the owner but couldn't reach him. While this was going on, Duke and I walked through the marina and studied the layout. Something crooked was going on here.

I saw boats like mine in the same condition. It looked like the mechanical work wasn't getting done. Perhaps they'd lost their mechanic. Or maybe they'd taken on too much work. Whatever it was, they'd drained $50,000 from my account and done nothing. I wanted someone's ass hanging up on a nail.

The next day, the owner arrived and assured me the work would be done properly and immediately. I decided to stay on the boat and watch them do the repairs. But my plans didn't work out.

Staying on the boat so near the swamp, the dank, nasty air affected my health. An open wound soon became infected with a fungus. With my weakened immune system, I was in trouble again.

Thankfully, I had good friends like Bill Reeves and Harold Mitchell. They drove straight to Mobile and loaded me and Duke into Harold's motorhome. Then they drove me back to Dallas for treatment. Bill followed behind in my truck.

By the time I arrived at Baylor Hospital, my right leg had swelled up. They diagnosed it as lymphedema, a potentially life-threatening condition. Once again, I would need months to recover.

During this time, I worked with my credit card company to back-charge the marina. The bank surreptitiously sucked out $50,000 from the marina's account. This caused a big explosion. Lawyers were called and lawsuits threatened.

I told the owner I was in the process of hiring local counsel in Mobile to sue them into bankruptcy. The owner paused, checked the cards in his hand, and decided to fold. We worked out a settlement where I paid them the original $30,000 and they would complete a long list of repairs. As a bonus, I demanded they transport the boat to Panama City, Florida. The idea was that by taking the boat that far, they (and I) would find out if it was seaworthy.

One clause in the agreement was that during my sea travels or otherwise, I wouldn't disparage the marina. I guess they wanted to have the ability to do the same thing to other unsuspecting boaters.

Meanwhile, I worked hard to recover back in Dallas. As always, Duke stood careful watch over me.

Somewhere during my recovery, I discovered that my sense of smell was gone. This was bad news for a sea captain. Not smelling leaking fuel or oil could be a death sentence. I would have to be extra diligent when examining the boat.

Once I was fully healed, Harold and I flew back to Mobile to check out the boat. The owner assured us the work had been done, so we demanded a short trip up and down the Intracoastal to set the GPS.

He provided a captain, and sure enough, he hit a submerged log, damaging the port side prop. They agreed to fix it at their expense.

During this same test run, the starboard side engine overheated. They sent the transmission to Ft. Lauderdale for an overhaul. When they got it back, it overheated again. I demanded they replace the thermostat and redo the cooling system. They agreed. I guess lawyers are good for something.

Months later, they pronounced the boat in first-class shape and scheduled a time to take it to Panama City. I loaded up Duke and went ahead, locating the marina where they would drop off the boat. During the few days I waited, Duke and I played in a park adjacent to the marina. It was fun watching him run off-leash across the grass, with not a care in the world. He seemed so happy.

One sunny afternoon, the captain arrived with the *Prima D*. I took it out with him and inspected the work. He assured me his trip down the Intracoastal had been fine.

"I ran it at normal speeds and made sure everything's working," he said. "You'll have no problem crossing the Gulf to Clearwater."

Because I found nothing amiss, I signed off on the delivery. Unknown to me, everything he told me was a lie. He had no problem sending me off with a broken boat. After all, if the boat sunk, who would know?

I watched the captain skip to a waiting car and take off for Mobile. Then I stared at my signature on the delivery slip. I had no idea I'd just signed my death warrant.

Chapter Seventeen

The *Prima D* rocked easy against a gentle swell. This made it easy for me to maintain a heading.

I studied the ocean and exhaled. Somehow, the pounding waves and high winds had abated. We just might make it.

I stared through the salt-pocked windshield, more in a trance than fully awake. Dead ahead, I thought I could make out the barest hint of dark gray in the eastern sky. Sunrise was close, as was land.

The gauge on the port engine told me it was still working. I could hardly believe it. It had held up, likely saving our lives.

I glanced down at the hole in my Croc. Duke had continually nipped at my foot, keeping me alert. I imagined telling this story in a bar somewhere, with most of the listeners whispering to each other that I had probably made it up. I would've done the same.

I thought back to everything I'd told my wonderful dog. Then I decided to make a confession. "You know, Duke, I've pretty much made a mess of the relationships in my life. I could've told Dad I forgave him instead of carrying this bitterness around. It's been like an anchor. A heavy, life-draining anchor."

Duke gazed up at me and said nothing.

"And I lost some great women too. Maybe if I hadn't been so career-oriented or drank so much, Beverley Bass wouldn't have moved on. And I know the bullying and drinking pushed Donna away. She was my last best chance for love. I blew it with her big-time."

Duke held my eyes for a moment then looked away. He agreed with me, but didn't want to say it out loud.

"It's been the same drinking that killed my brother, Gary. I can't believe I'm going to let it kill me too. I've got nobody left to love. I'm a single divorced man with nothing left to offer. No one's going to love me."

"I love you."

The voice shocked me. I twisted around to find the first mate's chair empty.

"And you have me to love," the same voice said.

Slowly, my eyes fell upon Duke. "What did you say?"

"I love you more than you can imagine," he said. "When you rescued me from that life of rummaging through trash and clipped the last painful bit of band from around my tail, I knew right then that I would devote my life to you. I never wanted to leave your side."

I rubbed my eyes to make sure I was seeing this clearly. "Oh my God, Duke, you're talking!"

"Animals talk to those they love. You just didn't hear me."

"I never heard one word," I said, stunned.

"You never heard me because you never believed you could hear me. You just needed to believe."

"Duke, I'm so sorry."

"There's nothing to be sorry for. I'm so grateful you made that effort to find the right food for me. No one else would've done that. I would've died for sure. You saved my life."

"I saved *your* life? I would've died at the foot of my stairs barely twenty feet from help if you hadn't barked your head off."

Duke nodded.

"And you've saved our lives by keeping me awake. By my count, you're ahead in the life-saving department. Don't you think?"

"I'm not keeping score," Duke said, "but I do want to say I'm sorry for pooping on the carpet that one time. I thought I could hold it until you came home, but I couldn't. I know you didn't get mad at me, but I felt real bad about that."

"I don't want you to ever worry about that again. It was nothing. I cleaned it up and we moved on."

He licked my calf.

I looked back out the windshield, spotting the first ray of sunshine peeking above the horizon. "We're going to make it, Duke. I can see land!"

"I knew you'd get us home. You're the best captain out there!"

I smiled and said nothing.

"And I want to make sure that I tell you that you're the best owner a dog could ever have. I love you."

Hearing that caused me to wipe away a tear. "You know, my father never told me he loved me."

"Well, I do. But I want to say something else before it's too late. Every dog knows that our master will have to let us go at some point. I don't know when my time will come, but I'm sure you'll do the right thing and let me go."

"You're all I've got, Duke. That's why I don't know if I'll be able to let you go. It's going to be hard. I'm hoping you'll be around for a very long time."

Duke touched me with his paw. "I'm getting older. I can't do what I used to. But while we can still talk to each other like this, I need to tell you that I want you to have another dog. If you want to get one before it's my time, I'd love that too—maybe show the pup the ropes, how my Captain likes his ship to be run."

I wiped my eyes again. "I just might do that. But promise me you'll stay as long as you can."

Duke said nothing.

"Promise me!" I said again. "Promise me you'll stay as long as you can."

A voice from below made me jump. "Stay after the boat trip is over?"

I blinked several times and rubbed my eyes. Duke was staring up at me, smiling. Behind him was Randy Cotter. "Tom, are you okay?

I heard you talking to someone and I thought it was me. Were you on the radio?"

"Uh... I just need a break. Can you hold the wheel?"

"Sure," Randy said. "Take all the time you need. Hey, I can see land!"

I patted Duke on the forehead and he licked me again. Then I made my way down to the cabin and collapsed on the bed.

Chapter Eighteen

As I stepped onto the dock, my knees almost buckled. I was so tired I needed days of sleep to recover.

"Did you folks just come off the Gulf?" a commercial boater asked me.

"Yes, why?"

"A twenty-five-knot wind out there led to a few rescues. Did you run into any of that?"

"You bet," I replied. "It was quartering off my port bow, trying to push us south. And with one engine, it was tough."

The boater shook his head. "You're lucky you made it. Other boats were pushed towards Cuba. If they ran out of fuel, we'll never find them."

The thought gave me shivers. I knew without a doubt that could've been me.

Randy and I unloaded the *Prima D* and secured her. With that done, I rented a car for Randy and sent him on his way back to Panama City.

I wanted to crash, but instead took Duke for a walk to a nearby field. He relieved himself several times. I could relate.

Duke took advantage of the shore leave and exercised hard, tiring himself out. By now, it was late afternoon. We were hungry. I fed both of us and checked in to a nearby motel. Then I collapsed on the bed without undressing.

The next morning, Duke was at my side as always, waiting for a command.

"Well, buddy," I said, "it's time to get our act together and get the old gal fixed."

Even though I'd been aiming for Clearwater, I'd ended up north at Tarpon Springs. By using celestial navigation, I had hoped to shift northward of Clearwater because it was a shorter trip. Sure enough, my navigation skills had worked. Yet the planned eleven-hour trip had taken more than eighteen. That's why I was so exhausted.

Calling around, I located a mechanic who had the ability to fix the engine. But he made it clear he didn't have the skill to repair any of the electrical issues. "You'll have to get that fixed in Ft. Myers," he said. "I can fit you in next week. I'll take it apart and see what I can find."

This meant Duke and I were free to explore the area. I rented a car and drove back to Panama City. We switched to my personal car and came back to Tarpon Springs. Then we went all over the place, exploring the area. We found fields, parks, and vacant lots. At each one, Duke ran with reckless abandon while I soaked up the sunshine. With all my health problems behind me, I needed a heaping dose of vitamin D—Mother Nature–style.

Many of the restaurants allowed Duke and me to sit on the patio. We spent many a morning having breakfast on a patio, gazing out over the water and watching the Gulf brighten as the sun rose behind us. We had a nice vacation.

After a few nights in a motel, Duke and I went back to the boat and stayed there. If I needed air conditioning, I could plug into the dock and be cozy.

Once the mechanic started working on the engine, he took up the flooring. Each night after he left, I had to put it back down so we could walk around. This was a lot of work, but I didn't have anything else to do. At least it forced me to get some exercise.

We spent six weeks in Tarpon Springs before the engine was finally repaired. What we discovered, though, was shocking.

"Look what I found," the mechanic said one day as he took me over to the boat.

"What is that?" I asked, seeing he was holding something in his hand.

"It's a bolt. It goes on the crankshaft, where the shaft enters the flywheel."

"It looks good to me. So?"

"It is good. I found it in the bilge. I think what happened was when they were repairing your boat, they accidentally dropped this and couldn't fish it out."

"What happened to the other four bolts?"

"They couldn't handle the torque, especially with the bad weather you experienced. Each one sheared off. Your engine worked; it just wasn't turning anything."

I stepped away from the mechanic and considered all this. It didn't take me long to figure out what had happened. The Mobile mechanic had accidentally dropped it and hadn't wanted to take apart the boat to get it. Or, he'd dropped it on purpose as a way to get back at me. Sure, they didn't have to leave it inside the boat for someone to find—but then I would've known for sure it was sabotage. By dropping it down there, they could claim it came loose, assuming there was a boat to inspect and people like me to complain.

But why didn't the remaining bolts shear off when they brought the boat from Mobile to Panama City?

Because they knew what they had done and ran the boat at idle speed. They didn't tax the engines. That's why they'd taken so long getting the boat to me.

Clever.

I discussed all this with the mechanic and wanted his opinion. "Yeah, I think that's what happened. Some of the marinas know you're just a transient boater passing through. Any mistake they make won't be found until you're long gone. I mean, what are you going to do? Turn around and demand they fix it? That's why some of them put a Band-Aid on it and charge you for a full surgery. You won't ever know the difference until it's too late."

He was right. And I was positive taking $50,000 from their bank account had not only pissed them off, but hurt them financially. They just had to get even.

It took several weeks for the mechanic to re-machine some of the engine parts. That's how much work it was to fix this boat. Eventually, he pronounced the engine properly repaired. I took it up and down the coast, testing it out. Sure enough, it worked.

Another problem that was fixed was the GPS plotter—or actually, the problem disappeared. Talking to people in the marina, I learned that most GPS plotters couldn't keep up with the fierce weather I'd endured. The constant recalculation between where the boat was at any given moment and the new projected route meant that it never had a time when the boat was simply on course. While it was crunching a new route, the boat had already drifted off course. Its brain wasn't fast enough. Driving in calm weather showed the plotter worked just fine.

With the *Prima D* running well, Duke and I decided to head down to Ft. Myers. I looked at the route and figured it would be a twelve-hour trip. Early one morning, I unhooked from the dock and eased off.

Hugging the coast and scooting into the Intracoastal made the ride smooth. My plotter worked fine, though I still didn't trust it. My VHF radio was still not working. I wondered why I hadn't spotted that when the dirty mechanic from Mobile had brought my boat to Panama City. Then I remembered that the long antennae had been pushed back flat to avoid scraping them on the underside of the many bridges. It was my fault I hadn't done a simple radio check before I took off from Panama City. As a former commercial pilot who'd continually gone through checklists, I should've done it. It had almost cost me my life.

Before taking this easy journey, I raised the antennae and did a radio check.

Nothing.

They still didn't work. Obviously, the antennae had nothing to do with it. I would have to get it fixed at Ft. Myers and rely solely on the handheld. It had a range of twenty-two miles—more than enough to reach land from any point along my journey.

I reached a point north of Ft. Myers with no problem. As I watched the sun dip below the horizon in the west, I couldn't wait to dock and eat a nice meal. Unfortunately, nature had other plans.

As I neared Useppa Island, a light fog rolled in. The visibility was still decent, but I worried it might thicken up. Flipping on the radar, I could see I was just east of Cayo Costa. The barrier islands to my west kept the Gulf waves down, but also blocked the wind from blowing the fog out. With each minute that ticked by, the fog grew thicker.

Going back to the radar, I tried bouncing beams off the channel markers. Since I could no longer see them, I hoped the radar would save me. It didn't.

I couldn't believe my luck. Here I was again, in trouble.

Faced with the choice of cruising along and possibly running into a boat or a rock or calling for Mayday, I had no choice. I reached over and hit the red button.

Nothing.

I had thought it was possible that the emergency button didn't work out on the Gulf because of the distance. Now I knew for sure it was broken.

I picked up the handheld and called out, "Mayday! Mayday! *Prima D* needs assistance. Lost in fog near Useppa Island."

A minute went by before a response came over the speaker. "*Prima D*, this is Captain Reynolds. I have your position. I'm calling the Coast Guard facility in Ft. Myers. Where are you headed?"

"To Cape Coral."

Silence.

More silence.

"*Prima D*. This is Captain Reynolds. I will be there in five minutes and escort you into Cape Coral. Be looking off your port side."

"Roger that. Many thanks!"

I stared into a blank wall of fog and saw nothing. Then, suddenly, he was right next to me. I had definitely made the right decision.

I followed Captain Reynolds in. He radioed, "Can you see the dock?"

"Not yet," I responded.

Captain Reynolds took me all the way into the marina and made sure I was tied up. After I thanked him, he turned his boat around and headed back out.

Later, I met Captain Reynolds on land. I learned that he owned an excursion boat. He had been heading out for a sunset cruise—a *paid* cruise. He told me he had asked the passengers if they wanted to help me or not. They'd voted, and I won. I didn't ask for the final tally. I didn't want to know how close I had come to disappearing in the fog.

"Can I give you anything?" I asked.

"No. We're good."

That was one solid guy.

The next day, I called America's Great Loop Cruisers' Association and learned about Kitty Nicholai. She was a Looper hostess, which meant I could take my boat through a series of canals to a dock behind her house and tie up. She had a bungalow where Duke and I could stay for free. In no time, Kitty and I became fast friends.

Like me, Kitty was an air and sea captain. Retired, she loved meeting new Loopers. And she was a great cook.

After settling in, I began the search for a mechanic to fix my electronics. I located a guy who scheduled me for two weeks out. After I was satisfied he could do the job, I found another dock—the Gulf Harbor Marina—and tied up there for the rest of my time in Ft. Myers. Kitty had Loopers coming around all the time, so I couldn't just park indefinitely at her place. Still, she continually invited me for dinner when she had new Loopers in. Despite my boat worries, I had a great time.

I had been in Ft. Myers for several weeks when I needed to fly home to visit my doctor. He planned on drawing blood and checking on my liver. I had to stay on top of my health. One more good illness and I'd be gone.

Kitty watched Duke while I was gone. Ten days later, I flew back and rented a car in Ft. Myers. I called Kitty from the car and told her I was on my way. She took Duke outside to the end of her driveway and said, "Daddy's coming." He perked up and stared expectantly down the road. I ran into some traffic and was slow getting there. When Kitty said, "Come on, Duke. Let's go inside," he refused to move. Instead, he lowered his body to the ground, resting his head between his paws, and continued staring. Nothing Kitty could say moved Duke.

She went inside and closed the door. Still, she kept a close eye on my best friend.

I was delayed by almost an hour. As I pulled onto the lane, there Duke was, waiting for his Daddy. And oh, was he happy to see me.

Kitty gave me a great report. "He's the best dog I've ever seen. So well-behaved and respectful. He practically watched himself."

I understood.

We enjoyed a nice dinner at Kitty's place, and Duke and I went back to the marina for a good night's sleep.

The next morning, the mechanic appeared. He informed me that the autopilot wasn't hooked up. Neither was the emergency button— the one that was supposed to activate my state-of-the-art VHF radio and send out a Mayday to the Coast Guard via satellite. He asked if I still had the box. "I need to see if there's a coaxial cable in there. That's why the systems aren't working."

I didn't have the box or the cable. When I told him about the past events, he said plainly, "This was sabotage."

With a bolt left off and a nonfunctioning emergency distress button *and* autopilot, the plan was for me to fall asleep so the *Prima D* could roll over and slip beneath the waves. But they hadn't counted on Duke.

A few days later, after checking out all the systems, the mechanic discovered that the radio antennae weren't connected. "Man, they sure did a number on you."

He had that right.

While we waited on parts to come in, I spent the lazy summer and fall days with Duke. I exercised him every day. He simply required it. And I loved doing it.

I learned from other boaters about a tiny island off Ft. Myers. Using binoculars, I could see it from the marina. Usually in the morning, after I had some breakfast and coffee, I would scan the island for any other visitors. If it was empty, I'd load Duke up in the dinghy and make the trip.

As soon as we hit the sand, he leaped from the bow and galloped off to take in all the fresh smells of a wild, untamed land. The island was a good quarter-mile long, if not more. Duke just ran and ran. Since he had filled up with plenty of water, he left his peemail everywhere. This allowed the other creatures to message him back. It was a good time for both of us.

We lived like this for six months when one day, the mechanic pronounced the *Prima D* ready. All the electronics had been fixed and engines checked over. I restocked the galley and hired a helper, a local mechanic who specialized in fixing toilets on boats. At least I had that covered during what was expected to be a two-day trip.

Duke and I made one last visit to see Kitty. We said our goodbyes and took off on the final leg of our big adventure.

The first stop was Marathon, a city about halfway down the Florida Keys. We reached Marathon the first day. The next morning, we left early and had an uneventful trip up the east coast to Ft. Lauderdale. I had already arranged a spot to park at a dock controlled by Jan and Mike Joyce, owners of Hargrave Custom Yachts. Not only did the Joyces build boats, but they acted as brokers to sell them. I was very fond of Mike and Jan. They had always treated me great, especially when I bought the second *Prima D* twenty-three years earlier. I wanted to find a good home for my old girlfriend. She deserved nothing less. And I knew without a doubt Mike and Jan would make sure she ended up in the right hands.

It was a cold December afternoon in Dallas. I stood at my patio door, watching Duke sniff around the backyard and take care of his business. I thought of the *Prima D* and the adventure I had endured to get her to Ft. Lauderdale. Most people would have sold her to someone on Lake Texoma and taken a serious price reduction. But I just couldn't do that. Too many fond memories. I just had to sell her to someone who cared.

It had been a week after dropping off the boat and returning home when the phone rang.

"Tom, it's me, Mike Joyce. Do you have a minute?"

"Sure. Did you find a buyer already?"

"No, but I have a strong potential. Listen, the reason I called was a title search. We ran one and found two liens on the *Prima D*—both from that marina you had issues with."

"What?!" I said, my blood pressure rising. "When did they file them?"

"A few months after you made that agreement."

I fumed. These guys were trying to back-door me, just like I'd done to them when I'd back-charged their credit card.

"Email me the liens. I have an agreement with these guys. I'll take care of it."

I hung up the phone and went to my filing cabinet. When I found the agreement, I read it again. Nobody who reads and writes English could doubt that we had settled the matter completely. One of the liens was for the transmission they'd damaged and repaired. The agreement clearly stated that was on them. The second lien was for the money they lost. Well, that too was clear. Everything was on them.

After I calmed down, I made the call to the marina and talked to the owner. He sounded surprised to hear my voice. I knew why.

I reminded him of the agreement and listened as he hemmed and hawed. He was using the threat of holding up my sale as a bargaining chip to extract some cash from me. I told him the next time he heard from me was when the judge ordered mediation. By that time, he'd be out $50,000 in attorney fees, *if* he was lucky enough to find an honest lawyer. Otherwise, the sky was the limit.

As he coughed and sputtered on the phone, I told him I had two mechanics ready to testify about the sabotage. He didn't even ask what I meant. Instead, once again he studied his cards and decided to fold. The two liens were removed.

Two weeks later, Mike Joyce called and said they had a buyer, cash in hand. The couple loved the *Prima D*, especially with all the modifications I had made for Duke. I had put in a special travel hoist for the dinghy that made it easy for a dog to get in and out. Many times, without a dock or marina nearby, the only way Duke could relieve himself was by taking him to land in a dinghy. The equipment I put in kept the dinghy level and steady so Duke wouldn't tip over as I raised and lowered it.

I'd also put in $6,000 worth of dog support equipment on the back end of that boat. Everything about the *Prima D* said "dog-friendly."

The new buyers wanted to close on December 28. Leaving Duke at home, I flew into Ft. Lauderdale and the Joyces picked me up. They insisted I stay at their condo. These folks were first class.

The next day, I went to the boat and discovered that the buyers, along with Mike's employees, had already boxed up most of my belongings and taken off all the furniture. That told me this deal was going to close no matter what.

I met the buyers and felt an instant connection. They were the right people for my old gal. And with a dog to roam about the deck, I couldn't have been happier.

We signed all the papers on December 28. I loaded up my belongings in a rental car and drove to Kitty's place, where I had parked my personal vehicle. After transferring the stuff to my car and returning the rental, Kitty treated me to a wonderful New Year's Eve dinner. The next morning, I said goodbye again and took off for Dallas.

I arrived on January 2, 2015, to a happy Duke. Donna had been taking care of him. He supervised the unloading of the car, making sure I didn't trip over anything. Since the weather had turned cold, I hustled the boxes inside to the living room floor. Once the car was empty, I made a fresh pot of coffee and sat down on the carpet with a steaming mug to start going through my stuff.

As I put things away, I found some old photos at the bottom of a box. As I studied them, memories of all the good times on Lake Texoma with Donna, the Corgis, and the other boating friends came flooding back. It was too much. I sat on the floor wiping my eyes. After a few minutes, Duke sauntered up, licking my face. He tried his best to comfort me. I put my arm around him and we just sat there for a while—two lonely guys missing our old girlfriend. At least we had each other.

Chapter Nineteen

The winter turned to spring and so did my thoughts. Everything was new, fresh, coming alive. I learned of a Texas breeder of Blue Heelers in New Braunfels. She had a fresh litter with three females. I had promised Duke a sister and wanted to make good on that. But I knew I couldn't drive a small puppy back home by myself. That's why I picked up the phone and called a good friend.

"Beverley. I need some help getting to and from New Braunfels."

"You're in luck," she said, laughing. "My daughter needs some flight hours for her logbook. I'm sure you can remember those days."

"I remember them well. Sign me up."

Beverley's daughter was named Paige. I offered to pay for the gas with a little extra for Paige's time. She agreed.

It was early May when I met Beverley and Paige at the Northwest Regional Airport in Roanoke. It was wonderful to see Beverley again.

"It's been so long," I said. "How are you doing?"

"Great. Still flying—private jets mostly. And how are you?"

"My health is a hit or miss proposition. Right now, I'm okay." I spotted a drop-dead gorgeous blonde standing behind her. "And who is this?"

"This," she said, pushing the girl forward, "is my daughter, Paige."

"Nice to meet you, Captain Tom," she said as she shook my hand.

Before we could say anything else, Beverley clapped her hands. "Let's get in the air, since that's where we all belong."

We climbed in her Piper Cherokee—a single-engine four-seater—and watched as Paige went through the preflight checklist.

Once the engine was at full power, she guided the plane down the runway and executed a perfect takeoff. In fact, every part of the flight was perfect. Paige was an excellent pilot.

During the trip, Beverley told me about her daughter's interest in flying. "Paige always saw me hanging around female pilots. When she was young, she couldn't even say the word pilot. Instead, she said 'pi-tot.' One afternoon, we were driving somewhere with her strapped into a car seat in the back. All of a sudden, I heard her say, 'Mom? Can boys be pi-tots too?' I couldn't even answer her. All I could think was how skewed her mind was. If she only knew what I had to go through to get my wings."

"If she only knew..." I agreed.

Once we were on the ground, I procured a vehicle to take us to the breeder. As the door flung open, we saw dogs and puppies everywhere. The breeder handed me a female a little over a week old. I held her for a while before negotiating a price and agreeing to come back when the pup was at least seven weeks old. With that done, Bev, Paige, and I flew home to DFW.

Two months later, it was time to go get Duke's new sister. I hopped in the Cherokee with Paige and Beverley and did a return trip. I cradled the puppy in my arms; she was precious. I figured since I already had a Duke, I needed a Duchess. That's what I named her.

From the moment Duke saw her, the change in him was profound. He was nine years old but acted like three. He bounded around the backyard with Duchess, a well of endless energy springing forth.

I watched him nudge his new playmate away from areas of the backyard that could have harmed her. He was both a patient dad and an enthusiastic playmate. I kicked myself for not doing this sooner.

Every guest I had over noticed the change in him. Clearly, Duke was in heaven. With everything we'd been through, I was grateful I could give him this.

It had been six months since Duchess had joined our household. Duke and I had always been the men around here, and it was nice to finally have some female companionship. As for me, my health had been back on the wane. I had undergone more back surgery and now needed an ablation on my heart for some Afib I was experiencing. I scheduled the day surgery at the Heart Hospital in Plano and arranged for Donna to drive me there.

Early that morning, I took a shower and got ready for Donna to pick me up. I stepped out of the shower and saw Duke coming to check on me—something he'd always done since my fall years earlier. Suddenly, he fell over sideways. I put down my towel and went over to pick him up, but he righted himself and was back on his feet. I assumed he'd just slipped, but deep in my soul I worried that it might be something more.

Once I was ready, I fed the dogs and prepared myself for the surgery. Donna arrived and walked through the garage door. Duke, hearing someone coming, went to check them out and make sure they were friends. Donna opened the door and spotted Duke. Immediately, he fell over.

"That happened earlier when I was coming out of the shower," I told her.

She picked him up and looked in his eyes. "Tom, can you drive yourself to the hospital? Bob and I will still pick you up. I think I should take Duke to the emergency animal clinic."

I rubbed my chin. "Yeah, I think you should do that now. I'll see you when I come out of surgery."

I drove to the Heart Hospital, worrying hard about Duke. That's why it was a relief to be put under anesthesia. My mind just switched off.

"Tom, are you awake?" It was Donna's voice.

"Yeah," I croaked.

"Good. They want to watch you for another two hours. Make sure you've recovered. Then Bob and I will drive you home."

"Okay," I said before promptly falling asleep.

Somewhere around two p.m., I found myself in the passenger's seat of my car with Donna driving. Bob was following in their car.

As the fog in my mind slowly lifted, I asked about my best friend. "How's Duke? What did the vet say?"

Donna hesitated, coughed, and started bawling. This caught me off-guard. Donna was usually the strong one—all business, the one with ice water in her veins. I could count on one hand the times I'd seen her cry. To see her like this, my newly repaired heart ripped apart.

"We have to see the vet, Tom. They don't know what's wrong. We may have to take him to a specialized clinic to do an EEG or something to find out what's going on."

My eyes teared up. The leftover anesthesia prevented me from getting too sad. I felt like I was in a nightmare.

I listened to Donna sob the rest of the way. When we arrived, she composed herself while I fell apart.

Once we were inside, the vet staff hustled us to an examining room. I wiped my eyes and Donna wrung her hands. After what seemed like forever, the door opened and a female veterinarian walked in. Her somber expression told me all I needed to know.

"Captain Toler, Duke has a cancerous tumor that's affecting his nervous system. We've got five different veterinarians in here who've examined him. After consulting together, we were unanimous: There's nothing that can be done for him. We recommend putting him to sleep."

I buried my face in my hands and let the tears flow. Her words were painful. Then I remembered Duke's words to me back on the boat: *I don't know when my time will come, but I know you'll do the right thing and let me go.*

Donna touched my arm. "Tom, we've got to let Duke go. It's his time."

Donna and I had been through so much. We'd seen so many Corgis reach their final day, endured a lot of heartache. She, more than anyone, knew the pain I was going through.

"Yeah," I muttered. "I promised Duke."

The vet coughed. "Captain Tom, we'll bring Duke in here and let you see him one last time."

The vet disappeared. Donna wrapped her arms around me, hugging me. I could do nothing but sob.

They carried Duke in and set him on the examining table. He looked terrible, with bandages on his legs from the lines they'd put into him.

"Could I have a minute alone with him?" I asked.

"Sure," the vet said, taking her assistant and Donna with her. When they had closed the door, I put my face next to Duke's.

"Buddy, we sure had some adventures together. I gave you the best life possible and you saved my life twice in return. No man ever deserved the love and devotion you gave me.

"I heard Donna talk about a special place pets go when they die. It's just this side of heaven. You'll be made strong again and get to run around all day. There are meadows, and large shade trees, and ponds to splash around in. And there are lots of new friends to play with. You'll have so much fun.

"One day, when my time comes, I'll be reunited with you. We'll hug each other just like we used to. And once we've calmed down, we'll walk over the rainbow bridge and be together—*forever*."

I rubbed his head, scratching his ears just like he loved.

"I'll say goodbye to Duchess for you. She'll be hurt for sure."

Staring into his pained eyes, I kissed his snout. Then I raised up and called the vet back in.

She carefully explained the procedure and proceeded with the shots. After a few minutes, she put the stethoscope to her ears and listened. She took the scope off and turned to me. "He's gone."

I nodded and let the tears flow. I had lost my precious Duke.

It was a month after Duke's passing before I felt better. I placed his ashes on my china cabinet, in a box. Below the lid sits a plate with his name and the date of death: September 21, 2016.

As for Duchess, she looked everywhere for Duke. She seemed hurt when I told her the truth. She continued smelling here and there, certain that he was hiding from her. But she never found him.

Sympathy cards poured in from everyone who had enjoyed Duke's company. I also received a bunch of Facebook postings. It didn't make the pain go away, but it did help.

I thought maybe one day I could hire Paige to take me over the Gulf so I could scatter Duke's ashes. Then I considered having his ashes spread over my grave. With my health problems, that's probably not too far away.

But I don't get too sad about that, because it just means I'm that much closer to seeing my best friend.

Isn't that right, Duke?

Photo Section

Big T, Mom, and
baby Tom.

Mom climbing into a Swift GC-1A.

Big T in the Navy.

Tom makes the paper with his first solo at sixteen.

THOMAS EARL TOLER
—Stone's Studio Photo

RH soph solos
on 16th birthday

A Richland High S c h o o l, sophomore had reason for a d u a l celebration Thursday, March 14.

He observed his 16th birthday and soloed both during the day and at night after completing flight school.

The feat, particularly the night solo flight at the age of 16, earned a trophy from Cessna Aircraft for Thomas Earl Toler and space in the company's magazine.

Hadley Sieberling, a Richland Hills resident, was instructor for Toler, son of Mr. and Mrs. T. W. Toler, 4801 Strummer D r i v e in North Richland Hills.

The young flyer soloed in his family's Cessna 172 after deciding three months ago to complete flight school and solo on his 16th birthday.

An h o n o r student, Toler had a quartet of A-pluses on his latest report card. The 190 pound six-footer played first string offense and defense on Richland's team during football season while maintaining his interest in flying and keeping his grades high. He was not permitted to solo before age 16, though he has been handling the controls while flying with his father since he was 10.

Now he plans to begin lessons in a multi-engine aircraft, an aero commander owned by his dad, who has amassed some 6,000 flight hours over the past 30 years.

The elder Toler is with Grimes Manufacturing Company, aircraft lighting installers with headquarters in Urbana, Ohio.

The Tolers' workhorse—a Comanche 250 with tail number 5686 P.

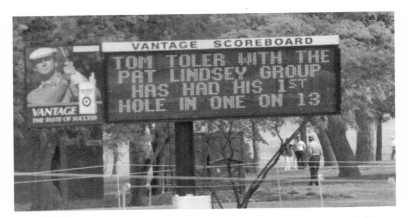

Tom scores a hole in one at the Colonial NIT Pro-Am Golf Tournament in Fort Worth, Texas.

Big T and Tom at the controls with Gary relaxing in the Tolers' twin-engine Aero Commander 560.

Shenandoah Oil's Learjet.

The photo that
Mr. Jimmy Stewart gave to
Tom during his time flying for
Shenandoah Oil. (Jimmy Stewart™
used with permission from The
Stewart Family, LLC.)

Photo by Harry Benson.

On their wedding day,
Donna looks on as
Tom putts out.

OUR LIFE TOGETHER
BEGINS THIS DAY

Captain Tom Toler.

Donna with her
two Corgis.

The first *Prima D* on Lake Texoma.

Tom with his father-in-law, Jim Ryan, playing in the Teesta Golf Tournament at the Great Southwest Golf Club.

The party scene at Lake Texoma.

Christening the second *Prima D*.

Donna with DFW TV news anchor Chip Moody.

Gary with Mom at her Euless home.

Duke in the backyard.

Special additions to the second *Prima D* for Duke.

The *Prima D* loaded for the trip north to Sallisaw, Oklahoma, and the Arkansas River.

Duke on the deck of the *Prima D.*

The famous Crocs
chewed on by Duke.

Tom cleaning the windows during the trip to Ft. Lauderdale.

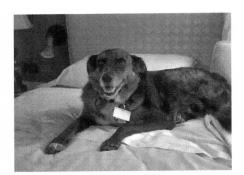

Duke relaxing on
the bed below deck.

The *Prima D* parked behind Kitty Nicholai's house
in Cape Coral, Florida.

The master bedroom of the second *Prima D*.

Tom and the *Prima D* make it to Ft. Lauderdale.

The uninhabited island off Ft. Myers where Duke ran free.

Beverley Bass with her daughter, Paige, and Duchess.

Duke and Duchess.

The adventurous route of the *Prima D.*

Epilogue

After I returned the *Prima D* to Hargrave Custom Yachts, Mike Joyce autographed a special book for me. I wanted to include what he wrote:

Dear Tom,

I hope you will enjoy reading a story of Jack Hargrave, who played such an important role in the boat business. I was only trying to write a book about Jack, when he died in the middle, and next thing you know I own the company and created the Hargrave brand. I am thankful that you brought the Prima D to us to sell. It really gave me a sense of pride that you came home to us and allowed us to have a sense of closure. My prayer for you is that God will allow this next chapter in your story to be one of your best, filled with new adventures and wonderful memories.

Mike Joyce and everyone at Hargraves.

As I read the final version of this book, I couldn't believe the vivid journey described in these pages. It was mine!

As you know by now, my story is one of an imperfect man leading an even more imperfect life. I wish I could go back and change some things, especially my behavior toward the ones I love and loved. But I can't. Life only goes forward, not backward.

To those I hurt, I can only offer a sincere apology. I hope you can forgive me.

Through my life, one person has been there to help me through the rough patches—Donna. Lately, she has taken up the role of "caretaker," coming over each day to see if I'm okay, making sure I get to doctors' appointments, and taking care of Duchess during my hospital stays. And she does all this out of unselfish love. Add in the fact that she's my ex-wife, and it becomes even more amazing. Truly, Donna is my guardian angel. I'm sure I would not be here without her love and support.

Donna also encouraged me to tell this story. She gently pushed me and kept track of its progress. Again, this book would not have been completed without her.

Then there's Duke. During that dangerous crossing, we bonded even more—if that was possible. We prayed together when all looked lost. We cried together when we saw land. We talked a lot, as reflected in the story. I had a completely different understanding of animals after surviving that trip.

Today, people post videos on YouTube, Instagram, and Facebook, showing animals helping each other and us humans. Recently, I saw a video that showed a large stingray presenting its eye to a diver. It did this over and over until the diver saw two fishhooks embedded just below the lid. He removed the hooks—no doubt causing great pain to the stingray—and set it free. However, the ray hung around the diver like it had found a new friend—or parent. I can't explain this behavior or even Duke's, but I do believe we have a duty to care for the animals God has placed in our charge. I hope my story has helped make that clear to all of us.

Finally, during that trip, I promised Duke a home with a backyard and a sister. I delivered on my end of the bargain, though only for six months before he died. But what a wonderful six months it was!

I still miss him. And I used a few tissues while going through this book. I'm pretty sure you did too.

I wish you the best.

Captain Tom

Author Bio

After twenty-eight good years with American Airlines, Captain Tom Toler retired in 2004. In 2006, the U.S. Coast Guard swore him in when he earned his Master of Steam or Motor Vessels of not more than 100 Tons Upon or Near Coastal Waters. He spent the next ten years traveling all over America's lakes, rivers, and coasts. After fifty years of life in the skies and on the water, Captain Tom came back to land where he spends his time giving speeches and meeting with book clubs and other groups. You can contact Captain Tom at CaptainTomToler@gmail.com.

Made in the USA
Monee, IL
08 October 2021